Burgers

Burgers

Classic American Hamburgers and Their Accompaniments

By Marcel Desaulniers

(Author of *Death by Chocolate*) and the American Burger Masters

PRION

A KENAN BOOK

Published in the United Kingdom in 1995 by
PRION,
an imprint of Multimedia Books Limited,
32-34 Gordon House Road, London NW5 1LP

A catalogue record for this book is available from The British Library.

ISBN 1 85375 185 5

10 9 8 7 6 5 4 3 2 1

BURGERS
Classic American Hamburgers and Their Accompaniments
was prepared and produced by
Kenan Books, Inc.
15 West 26th Street
New York, New York, 10010

US Editors: Dana Rosen and Benjamin Boyington
UK Editor : Beverly Le Blanc
Art Director/Designer: Jeff Batzli
Photography Director: Christopher C. Bain
Food Stylist: Roscoe Betsille
Prop Stylists: Leslie Defrancesco and Margaret Braun

Typeset by Classic Type Inc.
Colour separations by Fine Arts Repro House Co. Ltd.
Printed and bound in China by Leefung-Asco Printers Ltd.

ACKNOWLEDGMENTS

No cookery book is complete without saying thank you. Without the tireless assistance and co-operation of legions, this book would not be in print. So thank you to:

My wife, Connie, for her patience and love.

Ferdinand Metz, president of The Culinary Institute of America, for being supportive of this project and for his exemplary leadership.

The forty-seven Burger Meisters, for their creativity, their time and their energies.

My partners, for enthusiastically supporting yet another philanthropy.

Trellis Assistant Chef Jon Pierre Peavey, my right-hand man through this whole project. J. P. served as the chief burger recipe tester for *Burgers.*

Trellis Pastry Chef John Twichell, who, as the chief bread tester, once again lent his invaluable expertise to the creation of a cookery book. (John was also chief recipe tester for *Death by Chocolate.*)

Trellis Chef Andrew O'Connell, for his friendship and never-ending hard work.

Penny Seu, that's three down!

Dell Hargis, director of Alumni Affairs at The Culinary Institute, for providing the necessary nudges.

My agent, Dan Green, for the concept and execution of *Burgers.*

Dana Rosen, my editor at Kenan Books.

All the great folks at Simon & Schuster.

Weber-Stephen Products Company—the Weber Performer Grill with Touch-n-Go Gas Ignition System is terrific.

DEDICATION

To The Culinary Institute of America,
Our Alma Mater

FOREWORD

For this book, forty-seven prominent alumni of The Culinary Institute of America, the Burger Meisters, took time away from their normal routines (an oxymoron for most chefs!) to cook up the best burgers imaginable.

How does one gather such talent? Frankly, it was easy. The minute each chef heard that the purpose was to raise funds for our alma mater (the advance as well as all royalties go directly to The Culinary Institute of America), they offered unrestrained enthusiasm.

The Culinary Institute of America, located on a cliff overlooking the east bank of the Hudson River in Hyde Park, New York, is regarded as America's centre for culinary learning. An independent, not-for-profit educational facility and the only residential college in the world devoted entirely to the culinary arts, the institute has been called the Harvard of cooking schools. The institute will celebrate fifty years of culinary educational leadership in 1996.

**The Culinary Institute of America
433 Albany Post Road
Hyde Park, NY 12538-1499**

Contents

In his deliciously informative *The Dictionary of Food and Drink,* John Mariani, the distinguished chronicler of American foods, truly legitimised the subject of this cookery book:

> **Hamburger.** Also, "burger." A grilled, fried, or broiled patty of ground beef, usually served on a "hamburger bun" and topped with ketchup, onions, or other condiments. Hamburgers, along with hot dogs, are considered the most identifiably American of food items… The first appearance in print of *Hamburg* was in 1903… And soon the suffix *-burger* was attached to all sorts of other foods, such as lamb, chicken, clam… By the 1940s the hamburger was firmly entrenched as a quintessential American dish.

The variety of recipes for burgers contained in *Burgers* only reinforces Mr Mariani's words. Burgers are the favourite food of the hard hat on the construction project, the busy nurse on an all-night shift, the movie star on location, the executive after a few days in almost any foreign venue and most certainly the professional chef.

I am amazed at how often food conversations with my colleagues invariably turn from what is "in" to what is personally preferred. The food most widely proclaimed as the choice away from work is a burger, and as is evidenced by the recipes that follow, American chefs have not allowed their creativity to be restrained by simply relying on a ground beef patty, a bun and a bottle of ketchup.

Contemporary American chefs have staked a claim in culinary history by revitalising—not reinventing—American regional foods. Likewise, their burgers have been inspired by regional and ethnic pantries as well as local lifestyles.

From Phyllis Flaherty-Bologna's New England Maple Barbecued Pork Burger, served on an Anadama Roll and accompanied by Celeriac Chips, to Carl Walker's grilled Beef Burger, served on a Fresh Sage Tortilla with Piquant Avocado, *Burgers* illustrates the creative, delicious and exciting possibilities that burgers offer to the backyard barbecue cook as well as the professional chef.

Marcel Desaulniers
Williamsburg, Virginia

BURGER PREP

Master chefs, executive chefs, corporate chefs and chef-instructors. With this impressive group of food professionals, one would hope to find a consensus of information about burgers. We all certainly have a vast array of expertise and passion on the subject, but what we do not have are firm rules distinguishing the right way from the wrong way. Since so many variables exist when working with all foods, new and conflicting information is constantly appearing.

Burgers are like other foods in this regard. As soon as one learns that a certain method is the only method, along comes another expert touting his or her procedure. So what follows is excellent information that the next cook may choose to enhance, debunk or run with.

INGREDIENTS

With almost no exceptions, the ingredients in this cookbook are available in most major supermarkets or health food shops. Substitutions are not only allowed but encouraged, particularly for some of the uncommon ingredients, such as imported cheeses. The Duck Burger, for instance, is also exceptional using dark turkey meat. Almost all of the red meats are interchangeable; use pork rather than veal, lamb instead of beef. The Low Country Rabbit Burger would be quite delicious using chicken. Use hot or mild red and green chillies according to taste. The key element with any ingredient is quality and freshness—so always buy the best available.

Because fresh herbs impart subtle and specific flavours to foods, we recommend that they be used whenever possible. Although dried herbs may be substituted when fresh herbs are not available, their intensity of flavour requires that they be used with a very light hand. Another option is to substitute a more widely available fresh herb, such as parsley, when the specified fresh herb cannot be found.

RECIPES

All the recipes submitted by the American Burger Masters were tested at least three times. First the recipes were developed and tested by the Masters in their own kitchens. These recipes were then tested and adapted for home cooks by Jon Pierre Peavey and John Twichell at The Trellis Restaurant using equipment found in domestic kitchens. Adjustments were made, certain techniques were standardised and then the recipes were finally tested at the home of the author, Marcel Desaulniers. Marcel cooked all the burgers and accompaniments with Jon Pierre Peavey, and all the bread, bun and roll recipes were baked with John Twichell. The results of all this testing are recipes that are easily understood and that actually work. They also taste fantastic.

MISE EN PLACE

We had to use at least one "chef" term: *mise en place,* which literally means "to put in place". This term refers to the organisational method by which most chefs operate, whereby they organise, process, partially cook and in some cases totally prepare ingredients. This allows the cook to prepare recipes efficiently and as close as possible to the time of consumption.

In every recipe in this book, the list of ingredients is the *mise en place.* Prepare the ingredients prior to assembling the recipe (for example, roast, skin and seed the chillies) and you will have, in effect, the *mise en place.*

EQUIPMENT

As previously mentioned, all the recipes in *Burgers* were tested using domestic equipment, which means that everything needed to make the recipes is available to the home cook. Certainly, there are many enterprising people who make a living selling great gadgets that ostensibly make cooking just a step away from Nirvana. The truth is, if you have the passion for cooking, you can make do with or without just about any piece of equipment. However, certain tools do make life more enjoyable and burger-making easier.

CHARCOAL GRILL
The grill we used for recipe-testing is the Weber Performer Grill with Touch-n-Go Gas Ignition System. This kettle grill has an innovative system that allows you to light the wood or charcoal with the push of a button; a gas burner directs the flame on to the wood or charcoal, and within a few minutes you have "takeoff". Additionally, this grill has many features that make outdoor cooking essentially trouble-free. A variety of grills can be used to prepare the burgers in this book, from the widely used kettle grill to the economical and popular hibachi.

FLAT GRIDDLE (GRILL PLATE)
Some oven manufacturers offer the option of a flat griddle. Although not essential, this is a worthwhile feature if you have a large family or entertain a great deal. The griddle offers a cooking surface that is designed to sustain high temperatures as well as accommodate a substantial amount of volume.

FOOD MINCER
All recipes specifying "mince the food through a meat mincer fitted with a coarse mincing plate" were tested using the KitchenAid table-model electric mixer with a food mincer attachment. This sturdy piece of equipment makes this particular food chore a breeze. When mincing food, it is important to minimise heat generated by friction, and the powerful KitchenAid is designed with this consideration in mind. However, there are many other electric mixers or food processors with mincing attachments, as well as hand-operated mincers, that could also be used for mincing food.

JAPANESE TURNING SLICER
The manually operated Japanese turning slicer will cut seedless, solid-cored vegetables such as turnips, carrots, beets and potatoes into thin, seemingly endless strands. Look for the turning slicer in Asian food markets, or order one from a specialist kitchen supply shop.

LARGE NON-STICK FRYING PAN
The frying pan is economical, is easy to handle and clean and, more importantly, does an excellent job of conducting heat. The best is the aluminium-clad non-stick pan, which allows the cook to prepare foods with a minimum amount of fat; it can then be cleaned with a modicum of elbow grease.

Non-corrosive Containers

Foods with a high acidic quality should always be stored in containers made from a non-corrosive material, such as stainless steel or glass, to eliminate the possibility of a chemical reaction.

Stainless Steel Bowls

Although glass, plastic and ceramic bowls may be used for many of the recipes, stainless steel bowls have been specified because they are the most sanitary and safest containers available. Stainless steel also lasts a lifetime without breaking, chipping or cracking.

Making Burgers

Mincing Ingredients

Although this book has an eclectic and creative list of burgers, they almost always share one specific characteristic: whether made from beef, veal, chicken, duck, pork, tuna or prawns, the "meat" has been minced. The "meat" can be purchased and minced by the butcher, or it can be minced at home either by an electric mixer fitted with a mincing attachment or with a hand-operated mincer. The following list provides a few specifics about mincing food:

- Be certain the equipment is impeccably clean.
- Chill the food mincer before using, and always mince cold food. The colder the equipment and food, the less likely it is that the food will stick inside the mincer.
- Don't be a hero—always use the stomper to push the food being minced down the feed tube. Using the stomper ensures not only that all the food will be minced but also that you will retain your digits.
- Mince the food on high speed. A slow mince will likely mash the food and will affect the consistency of the burger.

- Thoroughly disinfect the equipment after every use. A good disinfecting solution consists of 1 tablespoon bleach per 900 ml/1½ pints of hot water. After it has been cleaned in soapy water, dip the equipment into the disinfecting solution and then allow it to drip-dry (do not towel-dry).

Combining and Forming the Ingredients

Ingredients should be treated gently when making burgers. The consistency and texture of a cooked burger depends, in part, on how it was treated in the preparation stages. Certainly, the ingredients should be mixed thoroughly to evenly distribute all components, but over-handling the food can result in a tough, dense burger. Using your hands is the most efficient manner in which to combine the ingredients for most burgers. Wear a pair of thin plastic gloves not only for hygiene reasons but also to prevent the combined ingredients from getting sticky. Form the burgers gently so as not to overly compact the meat. Handle gently and the eating will be easy.

Refrigerating and Freezing

Once the burgers are made, refrigerate them until they are to be cooked, preferably within twenty-four hours of assembly. Exceptions are the three vegetarian burgers, which can be refrigerated for two to three days before cooking.

Beef burgers oxidize quickly and start losing their bright red colour in a matter of hours. Freezing burgers is not recommended for the home consumer because most home freezers simply do not freeze foods quickly enough to retain quality.

COOKING BURGERS

Most of the burgers in this book are cooked over the open flame of a charcoal grill, cooked on a flat griddle or pan-seared in a large non-stick frying pan.

Weather conditions will probably be a factor in how you decide to cook your burgers. (Some of the burgers for this book were cooked on an outdoor grill during a snowstorm!) Whichever method you choose, the following list provides a few helpful tips:

- **Purchasing charcoal.** Hardwood lump charcoal is the best, as it burns cleaner and with more control than briquettes. It also burns very hot, which may not be a positive factor when cooking certain burgers. If hardwood charcoal is not available, then purchase a high-quality briquette. All the grilled burgers in this book were cooked over Kingsford brand charcoal briquettes; although most chefs prefer hardwood coal, we felt that for this book it was best to use what is most readily available.
- **Starting a fire.** The best method to start a fire is with a gas start. An electric fire starter is also an efficient and safe way to get your fire glowing. Although starter fluids are commonly used, we find them to be unsatisfactory for a variety of reasons, including safety concerns and unpleasant residual odours.
- **Understanding ventilation.** Air is an important factor in starting and controlling a fire. Fire needs a sufficient draught to feed its intensity and create good heat. On the flip side, too much air causes the fire to burn too quickly, leaving you with ashes rather than glowing coals. A grill with a cover helps control the fire. Covering the grill will limit the ventilation, and the fire will slow considerably. Removing the cover or opening all the vents will cause the fire to rage. Practise makes perfect.
- **Placement of the charcoal.** The shape or structure of the coals on the charcoal grate plays a significant role in the development of the fire. Try stacking the coals in a pyramid shape; this concentrates the heat in the core of the pile and improves the chances of a successful start.

Once the coals are intensely hot in the centre of the pyramid, spread them out. Then place the cooking grate over the fire (it is a good idea to leave the grate off until a few minutes before cooking; this allows for better access to the coals, and it prolongs the life of the grate).

- **Cleaning the grill.** Successful grilling depends on a clean cooking grate. Use a wire brush to remove food residue from the grate. Clean the grate with a damp towel, then wipe it with a towel that has been dipped in vegetable oil. The grate cleans easier when it is hot, so clean it immediately following cooking. Repeat the cleaning procedure just before cooking.
- **Medium wood or charcoal fire.** Most burgers should be cooked over a medium fire (turkey and pork burgers are more successfully prepared over a low fire). A medium fire is more easily observed than described, but generally speaking, a medium fire has coals that are red with grey edges. When the coals are intensely red, the fire is too hot; white coals mean the fire is on its way out.
- **Other methods of cooking.** As previously mentioned, most burgers in this book can be cooked on a flat griddle or in a large non-stick frying pan. Although the romance and the flavour of the fire are not present, results are usually excellent and in some instances even more desirable. For example, the Salmon Burger would be a mess to barbecue, and others, such as the New England Maple Barbecued Pork Burger, are more easily controlled on a griddle or in a pan.
- **Searing the burgers.** The debate is ongoing about the benefits of quickly searing, and supposedly sealing in the juices of, certain meats and certain burgers. The issue is still open to debate.

When it comes to burgers, there are so many variables that only personal experience seems to confirm the best method. So be brave and experiment. Just don't be foolish and get the fire too hot. (I did just that on opening day of The Trellis in November 1980, setting off the fire suppressant system and almost cancelling the opening festivities!)

USEFUL TECHNIQUES

ALLOWING THE DOUGH TO RISE

With many yeast-raised breads, the dough is allowed to rise until doubled in size. This procedure is called "proving". Proving is best accomplished in a fairly warm location (between 21°C/70°F and 27°C/80°F) away from draughts, and the specific proving times in this book were established in such an environment. Longer proving may be required if ambient temperatures are cooler.

COOLING FOODS IN AN ICE-WATER BATH

This quick method of cooling heated foods such as sauces and relishes involves placing the container holding the hot food into an ice-water bath. This bath may be a larger pan, a kitchen sink or any other container that will hold sufficient ice water to reach midway up the container holding the hot food. Stir the hot food frequently so that it will cool rapidly. This procedure will not only cool food, it will also inhibit the production of food-borne bacteria.

PEELING AND SEEDING A TOMATO

To peel and seed a tomato, first core the stem end with a sharp paring knife. Then, using the same knife, score the opposite end of the tomato by cutting a shallow X into the skin. Drop the tomato into boiling water for 30 to 60 seconds, depending upon the ripeness of the tomato (the riper the tomato, the shorter the time in the water). Retrieve the tomato from the boiling water with a slotted spoon and immediately plunge into ice water. When the tomato is cool enough to handle, remove it from the water and peel the skin away with a paring knife, starting from the X. Next, cut the peeled tomato in half horizontally. Gently squeeze each half under cool running water, allowing the water to flush away the seeds. The tomato may be stored tightly covered in the refrigerator for two to three days.

STONING AND PEELING AN AVOCADO

To stone and peel an avocado, use a sharp knife to cut the avocado through to the stone from end to end and all the way round. Gently twist the two halves of the avocado apart. Gently twist the stone free from the avocado by inserting the heel of the blade of a knife about 0.5 cm/ 1/4 in into the stone, then giving the knife a slight turn and lifting the stone away from the fruit. Peel the skin from the avocado using a thin-bladed paring knife.

PREPARING CHILLIES AND PEPPERS

To roast, skin and then seed chillies or peppers, begin by charring the skin completely black. Charring can be done by holding the chilli or pepper by the stalk over a gas flame using a pair of metal tongs, placing the chilli or pepper directly on to an electric range element or placing the chilli or pepper on the grill rack—also called the cooking grate—of a charcoal or wood fire. Turn the chilli or pepper frequently while charring to uniformly char and blister the skin.

To remove the skin, rinse the charred chilli or pepper under running water. Pull the stalk loose. Cut the chilli or pepper in half lengthways, then rinse each half under running water to remove the seeds. The chilli or pepper may now be very finely chopped, cut in strips or whatever other preparation the recipe requires. When working with chillies, avoid unpleasant skin irritations by handling with care. Use plastic gloves or wash hands immediately following the above procedures.

The Burgers

Bistro Burger
with Marinated Plum Tomatoes, Black Olive and Sun-dried Tomato Bread and Shoestring Potatoes and Frizzled Onions

Makes 4 burgers

Alison Awerbuch

Corporate Executive Chef and Partner
Abigail Kirsch at Tappan Hill
Tarrytown, New York

AT THIS EXCLUSIVE CATERING FACILITY AND RESTAURANT OVERLOOKING THE HUDSON RIVER IN HISTORIC TARRYTOWN, NEW YORK, CHEF ALISON AWERBUCH DRAWS HER INSPIRATIONS FROM AN IDYLLIC LOCUS THAT MARK TWAIN ONCE CONSIDERED FOR RESIDENCE. (ALTHOUGH TWAIN PURCHASED TAPPAN HILL, HE NEVER REALISED HIS DREAM OF LIFE ON THE HILLTOP; PERSONAL BANKRUPTCY INTERVENED, AND HE WAS FORCED TO SELL BEFORE HE COULD MOVE IN.)

ALISON CREATED THE BISTRO BURGER AT THE REQUEST OF A CELEBRITY CLIENT WHO WANTED TO SATISFY HER HUSBAND'S BIRTHDAY WISH FOR AN ENTREE THAT WOULD EVOKE THE FLAVOURS OF HIS TWO FAVOURITE FOODS—BURGERS AND PIZZA!

> *If the goat's cheese stuffing is not to your taste, try fresh mozzarella or even a Boursin cheese. You may also wish to vary the chopped fresh herb; tarragon, for instance, would work particularly well with the sweetness of Boursin, and fresh oregano might be just the right touch with mozzarella.*

4 whole shallots, unpeeled
6 cloves garlic, unpeeled
1 tablespoon olive oil
Salt and pepper
750 g/1½ lb lean minced sirloin
1 tablespoon Dijon mustard
1 teaspoon salt
50 g/2 oz fresh goat's cheese, broken or cut into small pieces

1 tablespoon chopped fresh basil
4 teaspoons coarsely ground black pepper
50 g/2 oz Parmesan cheese, shaved
4 fresh basil leaves

Preheat the oven to 160°C/325°F/Gas 3.

Cut the shallots into quarters (do not peel). Place the shallots and garlic on a baking tray, sprinkle with the olive oil and lightly season with salt and pepper. Cover the baking tray with aluminium foil. Place in the oven and roast the shallots and garlic for 30 minutes. Remove the shallots and garlic from the baking tray and cool for a few minutes.

Peel the shallots and garlic, then chop the pulp and place into a large stainless steel bowl. Add the minced beef, mustard and 1 teaspoon salt. Gently but thoroughly combine the ingredients.

Gently form the minced beef mixture into eight 75 g/3 oz patties, each 1 cm/½ in thick.

Use a metal spoon to make a small, shallow indentation in the centre of 4 of the beef patties. Equally divide the goat's cheese and chopped basil into the indentations, then top each with another patty and gently form into a burger, making sure to seal all open edges. Evenly sprinkle 1 teaspoon coarsely ground black pepper over each burger. Cover the burgers with cling film and refrigerate until needed.

Grill the burgers over a medium wood or charcoal fire. Cook until done as desired: 4–5 minutes on each side for rare, 6–7 minutes on each side for medium and 9–10 minutes on each side for well done. (This burger may also be cooked on a lightly oiled flat griddle or in a large non-stick frying pan over a medium–high heat. Cook for about the same amount of time as listed for grilling.)

Toast 8 slices Black Olive and Sun-dried Tomato Bread on the grill or griddle or in a non-stick frying pan until golden brown.

Serve the burgers on the toasted bread. Top each burger with Marinated Plum Tomatoes, shaved Parmesan and a whole basil leaf. Serve immediately with Shoestring Potatoes and Frizzled Onions.

Marinated Plum Tomatoes

Serves 4

4 plum tomatoes, washed, cored, cut in half, seeded and cut into 0.5 cm/¼ in pieces
2 tablespoons extra-virgin olive oil
Salt and freshly ground black pepper

When the warmth of the sun can be savoured with every bite of a vine-ripened tomato, you are experiencing a fruit that has just recently been plucked from the garden. If the tomatoes on hand are of this quality, you may wish to dispense with marinating them altogether. On the other hand, if the tomatoes are a bit firm and lacking in succulence, consider adding a splash of red raspberry wine vinegar to the marinade and allowing them to sit for several hours at room temperature before serving.

Thoroughly combine all the ingredients in a stainless steel bowl or another non-corrosive storage container. Cover with cling film and allow to stand at room temperature for at least 1 hour before serving.

Black Olive and Sun-dried Tomato Bread

Makes 2 loaves
(sixteen 1 cm/½ in slices)

1 tablespoon sugar
125 ml/4 fl oz warm water
1½ teaspoons dried yeast
125 ml/4 fl oz milk
350 g/12 oz plain flour
50 g/2 oz black brine-cured olives, stoned and chopped
65 g/2½ oz Parmesan cheese, freshly grated
75 g/ 3 oz yellow cornmeal
25 g/1 oz sun-dried tomatoes, chopped
1½ tablespoons olive oil
1 tablespoon chopped fresh oregano (or 1 teaspoon dried)
2 teaspoons freshly ground black pepper
1 teaspoon salt
1 teaspoon vegetable oil

In the bowl of an electric mixer, dissolve the sugar in the warm water. Add the yeast and stir gently to dissolve. Allow the mixture to stand and foam for 2-3 minutes, then add the milk.

Place the mixing bowl on an electric mixer fitted with a dough hook. On top of the yeast and milk mixture, add half the flour, the olives, Parmesan, 25 g/1 oz of the cornmeal, sun-dried tomatoes, olive oil, oregano, pepper and salt. Combine the ingredients on a low speed, then gradually add 125 g/4 oz additional flour. Once the additional flour has been added, scrape down the sides of the bowl. Mix on a low speed for 45 seconds, then once again scrape down the sides of the bowl. Continue to mix on a low speed 30-45 seconds until the dough begins to form into a ball. (If a table-model electric mixer is not available, follow the directions using a hand-held mixer or kneading by hand. The mixing times will increase depending upon which alternative method is used.)

Lightly flour a clean work surface, using the remaining flour as necessary. Knead the dough on the floured surface for 2-3 minutes. Cover the dough with a tea towel and allow to sit for 10-15 minutes. Once again, knead by hand on a floured work surface 8-10 minutes until the dough is smooth and elastic.

Lightly oil a stainless steel bowl with the vegetable oil. Place the kneaded dough into the bowl and wipe the bowl with the dough. Cover the bowl with a towel. Allow the dough to rise in a warm location about 1½ hours or until it has doubled in size.

Preheat the oven to 180°C/350°F/Gas 4.

When the dough has doubled in size, knock it back to its original size. Divide the dough into 2 equal portions. Knead each portion into a round loaf, about 12 cm/4½ in across and 6 cm/2½ in tall. Transfer the loaves to a baking tray that has been sprinkled with the remaining cornmeal. Cover the loaves with a dry towel. Allow the loaves to rise in a warm location about 45 minutes or until doubled in size.

Remove the towel and bake the loaves for 30-35 minutes. To test if they are baked, lightly tap the base of the baked loaves; a hollow sound will indicate that the bread is done. Remove the baked loaves from the baking tray and allow to cool to room temperature before slicing.

> *Alison loves her herb garden and suggests that if you are so inclined, many other fresh herbs would also work with this bread. Basil, which is delightfully abundant during the summer, and fresh thyme would both be delicious in this bread.*

Shoestring Potatoes and Frizzled Onions

Serves 4

Vegetable oil for deep-frying
5 large potatoes, such as Maris Piper, peeled and covered with cold water
65 g/2½ oz plain flour
¼ teaspoon salt
⅛ teaspoon ground white pepper
1 large onion (about 350 g/12 oz), peeled, cut in half and thinly sliced
Salt and pepper

Heat the vegetable oil in a deep-fat fryer (or high sided, heavy-based saucepan) fitted with a deep-frying basket over high heat to a temperature of 165°C/330°F. Preheat the oven to 225°F/110°C/Gas ¼.

Use a mandoline or a cook's knife to cut the potatoes lengthways into thin strips, about 0.5 cm/¼ in wide and 0.5 cm/¼ in thick. Place the potato strips in a colander and rinse thoroughly under cold running water until the starch has been removed from the potatoes and the water runs clear.

Use kitchen paper to pat the potato strips *very* dry. Remove the deep-frying basket from the deep-fat fryer. Place no more than one-sixth of the potato strips in the basket, then insert the basket in the fryer and fry the potatoes for about 4 minutes until they are a uniformly golden colour. (Constantly shake the deep-frying basket, or use a skimmer, to disperse the potatoes in the hot oil while fry-

ing.) Transfer the fried strips to kitchen towels to drain. Repeat the frying procedure until all the potatoes have been fried, waiting 1 minute before frying each new batch to allow the oil to return to 165°C/330°F.

Increase the temperature of the oil to 185°C/360°F.

Refry the potatoes, one-third at a time, 45-60 seconds per batch or until the potatoes are golden brown and crisp. Drain the potatoes on kitchen towels. (This second frying finishes the cooking process and makes the potatoes very crispy.) Keep the refried potatoes warm in the oven while frying the onions.

Lower the temperature of the oil to 165°C/330°F.

Thoroughly combine the flour, ¼ teaspoon salt and ground white pepper. Coat the onion slices evenly and lightly with the seasoned flour. Place half of the onions in the deep-frying basket, shake the basket gently to remove any excess flour from the onions, then insert the basket in the fryer and fry the onions until they become golden brown. Transfer the onions to kitchen towels to drain. Fry the remaining onions in the same manner. (Keep the first batch of fried onions warm in the oven while frying the remainder.)

Combine the fried shoestring potatoes and the fried onions, lightly season with salt and pepper, and serve immediately.

This recipe yields 4 large portions. The method to that madness will be quite obvious once you start eating Alison's addictive pairing of spuds and onions.

Wahoo Burger

with Asian-style Salad and Wasabi Mayonnaise

Makes 4 burgers

Benjamin Barker
Chef/Proprietor
Magnolia Grill
Durham, North Carolina

FOR MANY, THE DREAM OF A LIFETIME IS TO HAVE ONE'S OWN BUSINESS. FOR BEN BARKER, IT WAS TRULY A DREAM COME TRUE WHEN HE OPENED THE MAGNOLIA GRILL WITH HIS WIFE, KAREN, IN 1986. (KAREN IS ALSO THE PASTRY CHEF.)

BACK IN THE REAL WORLD, WHERE DREAMS HAPPEN ONLY WITH HARD WORK, BEN HAD "PAID HIS DUES" AT TWO OF THE BEST KITCHENS IN NORTH CAROLINA: LE RESIDENCE IN CHAPEL HILL AND THE FEARINGTON HOUSE IN PITTSBORO. AT THESE ESTABLISHMENTS, HE FINE-TUNED HIS CRAFT AND DEVELOPED THE CULINARY STYLE THAT NOW MAKES HIS MAGNOLIA GRILL ONE OF THE MOST POPULAR RESTAURANTS IN THE REGION.

BEN'S ECLECTIC STYLE OF CROSS-CULTURAL COOKING IS EPITOMISED IN HIS WAHOO BURGER RECIPE.

2 tablespoons sugar
4 circles rice paper (see Note)
750 g/1½ lb fresh wahoo fillet, cut into 2.5 cm/1 in pieces (or 750 g/1½ lb minced wahoo fillet; see Note)
2 serrano chillies, stalks removed, seeded and finely chopped (see Note)
1 tablespoon chopped fresh basil
1 tablespoon chopped fresh coriander
Finely grated rind of 1 lime
1 teaspoon chopped fresh mint
1 teaspoon finely chopped garlic
1 teaspoon grated fresh ginger
1 teaspoon fish sauce (see Note)
1 teaspoon salt
1 teaspoon ground white pepper
1 tablespoon groundnut oil

In a large stainless steel bowl, dissolve the sugar in 2.1 litres/3½ pints warm water. Soak 1 circle of rice paper in the warm water for 1 minute. Remove the rice paper and keep in between sheets of wet kitchen paper. Repeat the procedure until all 4 of the circles have been soaked. Keep at room temperature until needed.

If using wahoo pieces, mince through a meat mincer fitted with a coarse mincing plate into a large stainless steel bowl. Gently but thoroughly combine the minced wahoo with the serrano chillies, basil, coriander, lime rind, mint, garlic, ginger, fish sauce, salt and pepper.

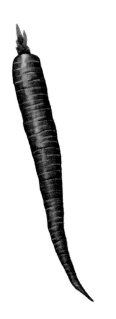

Gently form the ground wahoo mixture into four 175 g/6 oz burgers, each 2 cm/3/4 in thick.

Remove the rice paper from the wet kitchen towels and place each burger in the centre of a rice paper circle. Fold the rice paper over the burgers, forming a packet around each burger. Cover with cling film and refrigerate for at least 1 hour.

Heat a large non-stick frying pan that has been lightly brushed with the groundnut oil over a medium-high heat. Sear the burgers 6-8 minutes on each side or until golden brown and cooked through.

Serve the burgers with Asian-style Salad and a ramekin of Wasabi Mayonnaise.

Note: Rice paper is made from rice flour and water and can be found in Asian grocery shops. Primarily used for making spring rolls, rice paper gives the Wahoo Burger a wonderful crispy finish that makes a bun or a roll unnecessary.

Wahoo is one of the most prized fish available. It has a fine white flesh that belies its genus—the mackerel family. An adequate substitute for this recipe would be tuna fillets.

Serrano chillies are bitingly hot green chllies. If they are not available, substitute any small red or green hot chillies.

Asian fish sauces are very inexpensive condiments and are readily available from Asian and general supermarkets.

Asian-style Salad

Serves 4

4 tablespoons groundnut oil
2 tablespoons orange juice
1 teaspoon chopped fresh basil
1 teaspoon chopped fresh coriander
1 teaspoon grated fresh ginger
1 teaspoon chopped fresh mint
1 teaspoon light soy sauce
¼ teaspoon dried chilli flakes
1 carrot, peeled and coarsely grated (see Note)
1 small fennel bulb, cored and thinly sliced
   Salt
1 head frisée lettuce, cut into 2 cm/³/₄ in pieces, washed and dried

In a stainless steel bowl, whisk together the groundnut oil, orange juice, basil, coriander, ginger, mint, soy sauce and chilli flakes. The dressing may be covered and refrigerated for 2 or 3 days or used immediately.

Toss the carrot and fennel with the dressing. Adjust the seasoning with salt. Portion the frisée lettuce on to serving plates. Divide the dressed fennel-carrot mixture equally over the greens and serve immediately.

Note: The carrot may be prepared by grating in a food processor fitted with a medium grating disc.

Wasabi Mayonnaise

Makes about 225 g/8 oz

1 tablespoon wasabi powder (see Note)
2 tablespoons cold water
175 g/6 oz mayonnaise
   Juice of ½ lime
1 teaspoon finely chopped garlic
½ teaspoon soy sauce
½ teaspoon sesame oil
½ teaspoon rice vinegar
   Salt and white pepper

Reconstitute the wasabi powder in the cold water.

In a stainless steel bowl, whisk together the mayonnaise, wasabi mixture, lime juice, garlic, soy sauce, sesame oil and rice vinegar. Adjust the seasoning with salt and pepper, then whisk until smooth and thoroughly combined.

The mayonnaise will keep tightly covered in the refrigerator for 2 or 3 days.

Note: Wasabi (known as Japanese horseradish) powder is available in Asian grocery shops. Once reconstituted, it produces a very hot greenish-coloured paste. If wasabi is unavailable, prepared horseradish can be substituted to taste.

Sonoma Lamb Burger
with Grilled Golden Potatoes and Radicchio and Watercress Salad

Makes 4 burgers

Elaine Bell
Chef/Owner
Elaine Bell Catering Company
Sonoma, California

ALTHOUGH SHE PURSUED A DEGREE IN FOOD SCIENCE AND NUTRITION IN COLLEGE, ELAINE BELL'S DESIRE FOR A MORE TACTILE RELATIONSHIP WITH FOOD LED HER TO VENTURE TO HYDE PARK, NEW YORK. THERE, AT THE CULINARY INSTITUTE OF AMERICA, HER PHILOSOPHY ON FOOD EVOLVED.

LISTEN TO ELAINE TALK ABOUT HER BURGER RECIPE, AND YOU WILL UNDERSTAND WHY HER FOOD IS SO TASTEFULLY AND INTELLIGENTLY PREPARED:

SINCE I LIVE IN ONE OF THE MOST BOUNTIFUL FOOD AND WINE AREAS IN OUR COUNTRY, SONOMA COUNTY, I WANT TO SHARE A RECIPE THAT I FEEL CAPTURES THE TRADITION OF "WINE COUNTRY CUISINE". SONOMA COUNTY FARMERS PRODUCE WONDERFUL LAMB, SUN-DRIED TOMATOES, GOAT'S CHEESE, FRESH HERBS, VEGETABLES AND OLIVE OIL. THESE INGREDIENTS HAVE BECOME STAPLES IN OUR DAILY COOKING. MY LAMB BURGER COMBINES THEM INTO A TRUE SONOMA EXPERIENCE.

900 g/2 lb fresh lamb meat from shoulder, trimmed and cut into 2.5 cm/1 in pieces (or 900 g/2 lb minced lamb meat from shoulder)

2 tablespoons finely chopped flat-leaf parsley

7 cloves garlic (3 peeled and finely chopped)

1 tablespoon freshly ground black pepper, plus ¼ teaspoon

2 teaspoons salt, plus 2 pinches

1 teaspoon olive oil

125 g/4 oz fresh goat's cheese

6 sun-dried tomatoes, coarsely chopped

1 tablespoon toasted pine nuts

2 teaspoons chopped fresh basil

1 teaspoon chopped fresh chives

125 ml/4 fl oz balsamic vinegar Salt and freshly ground black pepper

Preheat the oven to 180°C/350°F/Gas 4.

If using lamb pieces, mince them through a meat mincer fitted with a coarse mincing plate into a large stainless steel bowl.

Gently but thoroughly combine the ground lamb with the chopped parsley, garlic, 1 tablespoon freshly ground black pepper and 2 teaspoons salt.

Gently form the seasoned lamb into eight 125 g/4 oz patties, each 2.5 cm/ 1 in thick. Cover the patties with cling film and refrigerate until needed.

Place the 4 whole unpeeled garlic cloves on a baking sheet and sprinkle with the olive oil. Roast the garlic in the oven for about 20 minutes until lightly browned. Transfer the garlic to a small plate and place, uncovered, in the refrigerator about 15 minutes to cool. Gently remove the peels from the chilled cloves of garlic.

Elaine does not serve her burger on a bun. If you are so inclined, a delicious pairing would be to serve the lamb burger on grilled focaccia (see page 82), brushed with extra-virgin olive oil and sprinkled with chopped fresh herbs.

In a stainless steel bowl, combine the goat's cheese, sun-dried tomatoes, pine nuts, basil, chives, remaining ¼ teaspoon freshly ground black pepper and remaining 2 pinches salt. Divide the mixture into 4 equal portions. Place 1 of the chilled, peeled garlic cloves into the centre of each portion, then form each into a smooth round ball.

Use a metal spoon to make a small, shallow indentation in the centre of 4 of the lamb patties. Place a goat's cheese ball in each indentation, top with another patty and gently form into burgers, each 3 cm/1¼ in thick, making sure to seal all open edges. Cover the burgers with cling film and refrigerate until needed.

Heat the balsamic vinegar in a small saucepan over a medium-high heat. Bring the vinegar to the boil, then reduce the heat and allow to simmer slowly for 10 minutes until the vinegar has been reduced to one-fourth its original volume (2 tablespoons). Remove from the heat and allow to cool.

Just before grilling, lightly season the burgers with salt and freshly ground black pepper, then brush them with the balsamic vinegar glaze. Grill the burgers over a medium wood or charcoal fire. Cook as desired: 4-5 minutes on each side for rare, 6-7 minutes on each side for medium and 8-9 minutes on each side for well done. (This burger may also be cooked on a well-seasoned flat griddle or in a large non-stick frying pan over a medium-high heat. Cook for about the same amount of time as listed for grilling.)

Serve the burgers with Grilled Golden Potatoes and Radicchio and Watercress Salad.

Grilled Golden Potatoes

Serves 4

4 potatoes, about 900 g/2 lb, washed
4 tablespoons extra-virgin olive oil
Salt and freshly ground black pepper
2 tablespoons finely chopped fresh chives

Preheat the oven to 200°C/400°F/Gas 6.

Pierce the potatoes 2 or 3 times with a fork. Bake the potatoes on a baking tray covered with aluminium foil for 50 minutes. Transfer to a plate and place, uncovered, in the refrigerator about 30 minutes to cool thoroughly.

Slice the chilled potatoes into 0.5 cm/¼ in thick slices. The sliced potatoes may be covered with cling film and refrigerated for up to 2 days before grilling.

Just before grilling, thoroughly coat the sliced potatoes with the olive oil and season with salt and pepper. Grill the potatoes over a medium wood or charcoal fire 3-5 minutes on each side until golden brown. Sprinkle the potatoes with the chives and serve immediately.

> *Many types of potato can be used in this recipe. The varieties most suitable for grilling include King Edward, Maris Piper, Romano and Desirée. No matter which variety you use, be certain to bake thoroughly and to chill the potatoes.*

Radicchio and Watercress Salad

Serves 4

6 tablespoons extra-virgin olive oil
2 tablespoons red wine vinegar
1 clove garlic, peeled and crushed
1 tablespoon chopped fresh flat-leaf parsley
½ teaspoon cracked black pepper
¼ teaspoon salt
1 large head radicchio, about 225 g/8 oz, cored, torn into 5 cm/2 in pieces, washed and dried (see Note)
1 large bunch watercress, stalks trimmed, washed and dried
2 tablespoons pine nuts, toasted

In a small stainless steel bowl, whisk together the olive oil, red wine vinegar, garlic, parsley, pepper and salt. Combine thoroughly. Cover and keep at room temperature for up to 3-4 hours. Just before using, whisk the ingredients to thoroughly combine and remove the garlic clove.

Place the prepared radicchio and watercress in a large bowl and drizzle over the dressing. Add the pine nuts. Gently toss all the ingredients together until the greens are lightly coated. Serve immediately.

Note: Radicchio's cabbage-like appearance has it frequently being mistaken for just that. Radicchio has a unique, subtle bittersweet flavour that sets it apart from cabbage—and other greens, for that matter. It can be found year-round, albeit of varying quality, in most supermarkets.

Chicago Beer Burger

with Beer-braised Onions and Mushroom Beer Ketchup

Makes 4 burgers

Carlyn Berghoff
President/Owner
Carlyn Berghoff Catering
Chicago, Illinois

CARLYN BERGHOFF IS A FOURTH-
GENERATION MEMBER OF ONE OF
CHICAGO'S BEST-KNOWN RESTAURANT
FAMILIES. HER GREAT-GRANDFATHER
OPENED HIS FIRST CAFÉ AND BREWERY
THERE IN 1898, AND TO THIS DAY THE
BERGHOFF NAME SIGNIFIES A WINDY CITY
INSTITUTION OF HEARTY FULL-FLAVOURED
FOOD AND HOME-BREWED REGIONAL
BEER.

WITH THIS HERITAGE IN MIND, CARLYN
AND EXECUTIVE CHEF DAVID NORMAN,
ALSO A CULINARY INSTITUTE OF AMERICA
GRADUATE, WERE INSPIRED TO CREATE A
BURGER AND ACCOMPANIMENTS THAT
ARE ALL TOUCHED BY THE BERGHOFF
TRADITION OF COMBINING GOOD FOOD
AND GOOD BEER.

> *For an attractive garnish, use a bunch of watercress with a few sliced raw mushrooms sprinkled with lemon juice.*

750 g/1½ lb minced beef
2 tablespoons beer
½ teaspoon Tabasco Sauce
¼ teaspoon Worcestershire sauce
Salt and pepper

4 slices, about 15 g/½ oz each, mature cheese (see Note)
4 Best Burger Buns (see page 109), cut in half

In a large stainless steel bowl, gently but thoroughly combine the minced beef, beer, Tabasco Sauce, Worcestershire sauce and salt and pepper to taste.

Gently form the seasoned beef into four 175 g/6 oz burgers, each 2.5 cm/ 1 in thick. Cover the burgers with cling film and refrigerate until needed.

Grill the burgers over a medium wood or charcoal fire. Cook as desired: 3-4 minutes on each side for rare, 5-6 minutes on each side for medium and 8-9 minutes on each side for well done. Top each burger with some of the Beer-braised Onions and then with a slice of the cheese and allow it to melt. If you have a cover for the grill, quickly melt the cheese by placing the cover over the grill for a few moments. (This burger may also be cooked on a well-seasoned flat griddle or in a large non-stick frying pan over a medium–high heat. Cook for about the same amount of time as listed for grilling.)

Toast the buns, cut sides down, on the grill or in a non-stick pan until golden brown.

Serve the burgers on the toasted buns with a ramekin of Mushroom Beer Ketchup.

Note: Strong-smelling German Limburger cheese or a mature Cheddar cheese are great for topping this burger.

Beer-braised Onions

Serves 4

15 g/¹⁄₂ oz unsalted butter
1 large onion, about 350 g/12 oz, thinly sliced
225 ml/8 fl oz beer
1 teaspoon sugar
¹⁄₂ teaspoon salt

Melt the butter in a large saucepan over a medium-high heat. Add the onions and cook, stirring frequently, for 5–6 minutes until they are very tender. Add 175 ml/6 fl oz of the beer, sugar and salt. Cook 16-18 minutes until all the beer has been absorbed by the onions and they begin to brown lightly. Add the remaining beer and bring to a simmer. Place on top of the Chicago Beer Burgers.

These onions can also be cooled and refrigerated until needed. Heat the cooled onions to a simmer before using. When the onions are hot, perk up their flavour with a splash or two of beer.

Mushroom Beer Ketchup

Makes about 350 g/12 oz

15 g/¹⁄₂ oz unsalted butter
1 small onion, chopped
125 g/4 oz mushrooms, stalks trimmed and sliced
75 ml/3 fl oz beer, hot
75 g/3 oz ketchup
1 tablespoon distilled white vinegar
¹⁄₄ teaspoon sugar
¹⁄₄ teaspoon salt

Melt the butter in a large saucepan over a medium heat. Add the onions and cook for 3-4 minutes until tender. Add the mushrooms and continue cooking for an additional 3-4 minutes.

Remove the saucepan from the heat and add the beer, ketchup, white vinegar, sugar and salt. Use a mouli, blender or food processor to purée the mixture until smooth.

Return the saucepan with the puréed mixture to a medium heat. Bring the mixture to the boil, then reduce the heat and allow to simmer for about 12 minutes until slightly thickened. Remove from the heat and cool in an ice-water bath. Transfer the Mushroom Beer Ketchup to a non-corrosive storage container and refrigerate for 24 hours before using. This ketchup will keep in the refrigerator for several days.

> *Although the Mushroom Beer Ketchup is a delightful addition to the Chicago Beer Burger, it also works well with a variety of other burgers as well as other grilled meats.*

 # Plymouth Turkey Burger
with Cranberry Relish and Country-style Mashed Potatoes

Makes 4 burgers

John Bowen
Executive Vice President
Johnson & Wales University
Providence, Rhode Island

GRADUATION FROM THE CULINARY INSTITUTE WAS JUST THE FIRST STEP IN JOHN BOWEN'S ACADEMIC INVOLVEMENT IN THE CULINARY FIELD. HE WENT ON TO COMPLETE HIS BACHELOR OF SCIENCE DEGREE AT JOHNSON & WALES UNIVERSITY, SERVED ON THE FACULTY THERE AND LATER EARNED A MASTER'S DEGREE IN MANAGEMENT.

BEFORE ASSUMING HIS RESPONSIBILITIES AS EXECUTIVE VICE PRESIDENT, JOHN WAS THE DEAN OF THE CULINARY ARTS DIVISION OF THIS RHODE ISLAND-BASED SCHOOL.

ALTHOUGH THIS TASTEFUL LOW-FAT BURGER RECIPE WAS NOT CARRIED OVER ON THE *MAYFLOWER*, THE PILGRIM "SPIRIT" OF ITS FLAVOUR IS SURE TO MAKE BURGER HISTORY.

15 g/½ oz unsalted butter
65 g/2½ oz onions, finely diced
2 cloves garlic, finely chopped
750 g/1½ lb boneless and skinless white turkey meat, cut into 2.5 cm/1 in pieces (or 750 g/1½ lb minced white turkey meat; see Note)
1 teaspoon salt
½ teaspoon ground white pepper
50 g/2 oz dry breadcrumbs
4 Best Burger Buns (see page 109) or other favourite buns, cut in half
4 tablespoons mayonnaise
Lollo rosso lettuce leaves, washed and dried

Melt the butter in a small non-stick frying pan over a medium heat. When the butter has melted, add the onions and garlic and cook 3–4 minutes until the onions are translucent. Transfer the onions and garlic to a plate and place, uncovered, in the refrigerator to cool.

If using turkey pieces, mince the turkey through a meat mincer fitted with a coarse mincing plate into a large stainless steel bowl.

Add the cooled onions and garlic, salt and pepper to the minced turkey, and gently but thoroughly combine.

Gently form the turkey mixture into four 175 g/6 oz burgers, each 2.5 cm/ 1 in thick. Cover the burgers with cling film and refrigerate until needed.

Preheat the oven to 160°C/325°F/Gas 3.

Place the breadcrumbs on a plate. Place the turkey burgers one at a time into the breadcrumbs and gently but thoroughly coat with the crumbs.

Heat a lightly oiled flat griddle or a large non-stick frying pan over a medium–high heat. When hot, cook the burgers for 2–3 minutes on one side. Use a fish slice to turn the burgers and to press down lightly on each. Cook the burgers for an additional 2–3 minutes. Place the burgers on a baking tray in the oven for 14–18 minutes until cooked through.

Toast the buns, cut sides down, on the griddle or in a non-stick frying pan over a medium-high heat for about 1 minute, until golden brown.

Spread each top and bottom bun half with mayonnaise. Garnish each bottom bun half with the lollo rosso leaves, then place a turkey burger on top. Top each burger with Cranberry Relish and the top half of the bun. Serve immediately with a portion of Country-style Mashed Potatoes.

Note: Although this recipe specifies white breast meat, feel free to substitute dark thigh meat or to use a combination of both. When using thigh meat, be certain to remove all the skin and tendons before mincing.

Cranberry Relish

Makes about 175 g/6 oz

1 crisp red apple
225 g/8 oz fresh or frozen whole cranberries
1 navel orange, peeled and divided into sections
100 g/3½ oz light brown sugar
75 g/3 oz clear honey
Pinch ground cinnamon
Pinch ground white pepper

Peel, quarter and core the apple. Immediately place the apple pieces and remaining ingredients in a food processor fitted with a metal blade and pulse for 5-8 seconds.

Heat the processed mixture in a large stainless steel saucepan over a medium-high heat. Bring the mixture to the boil, then adjust the heat and allow to simmer for 3-4 minutes, stirring frequently. Remove from the heat and cool in an ice-water bath. Transfer the cooled relish to a non-corrosive storage container and refrigerate tightly covered for at least 24 hours before using. The relish will keep in the refrigerator for several days.

> *For textural interest, consider adding 50 g/2 oz chopped walnuts to the cooled relish.*

Country-style Mashed Potatoes

Serves 4

900 g/2 lb potatoes, peeled
1 tablespoon salt
125 g/4 oz unsalted butter
50 ml/2 fl oz milk, hot
Salt and freshly ground black pepper

Wash the potatoes, then cut them into 2.5 cm/1 in pieces.

Place the potatoes in a large saucepan. Cover with cold water and add 1 tablespoon salt. Bring the water to the boil over a high heat, then lower the heat to medium and allow the potatoes to simmer for about 30 minutes until cooked through.

Drain the cooked potatoes in a colander, then place in a stainless steel bowl. Add the butter, milk and salt and pepper to taste. Mash the potatoes with a potato masher.

> *A totally indulgent and delicious substitution would be to replace the milk with double cream.*

Grilled Turkey Burger
with Fresh Tomato Sauce

Makes 4 burgers

Lyde Buchtenkirch-Biscardi

Team Leader for Curriculum
The Culinary Institute of America
Hyde Park, New York

EDUCATION HAS BEEN THE FOCUS OF LYDE BUCHTENKIRCH-BISCARDI'S CAREER SINCE SHE GRADUATED FROM THE CULINARY INSTITUTE OF AMERICA. FOR SEVERAL YEARS SHE SERVED AS A CHEF-INSTRUCTOR IN THE CULINARY ARTS DIVISION AT JOHNSON & WALES UNIVERSITY IN PROVIDENCE, RHODE ISLAND. IN 1978, SHE RETURNED TO THE CULINARY INSTITUTE AND HAS SINCE MADE SIGNIFICANT CONTRIBUTIONS TO THE SCHOOL.

LYDE'S IMPRESSIVE ARRAY OF PROFESSIONAL AWARDS AND ACHIEVEMENTS INCLUDES HER DESIGNATION AS THE FIRST AND ONLY WOMAN TO BE CERTIFIED A MASTER CHEF BY THE AMERICAN CULINARY FEDERATION.

THE ITALIANATE TWIST TO LYDE'S BURGER WILL HAVE YOU SAYING *CIAO* TO OTHER TEMPTATIONS.

5 tablespoons extra-virgin olive oil
1 teaspoon finely chopped garlic
1 teaspoon chopped fennel seeds
750 g/1½ lb boneless and skinless white turkey meat, cut into 2.5 cm/1 in pieces (or 750 g/1½ lb minced white turkey meat)

25 g/1 oz Parmesan cheese, freshly grated
1 teaspoon chopped fresh oregano
Salt and pepper
8 slices Focaccia (see page 82)
4 slices mozzarella cheese, each about 25 g/1 oz

Heat 1 tablespoon olive oil in a small non-stick frying pan over a medium-high heat. When hot, add the garlic and fennel seeds and cook for 1 minute. Transfer mixture to a plate and place, uncovered, in the refrigerator to cool.

If using turkey pieces, mince the turkey through a meat mincer fitted with a coarse mincing plate into a large stainless steel bowl.

Gently but thoroughly combine the minced turkey with the cooled garlic and fennel seed mixture, Parmesan and oregano. Season with salt and pepper.

Form the ground turkey mixture into four 175 g/6 oz burgers, each 2.5 cm/1 in thick. Cover the burgers with cling film and refrigerate for at least 30 minutes until needed.

Preheat the oven to 190°C/375°F/Gas 5.

Prior to grilling, brush the burgers with 2 tablespoons olive oil. Lightly season with salt and pepper.

Grill the burgers over a low wood or charcoal fire. Cook for 3 minutes on each side. Remove the burgers from the grill and place on a baking tray. (This burger may also be cooked on a lightly oiled flat griddle or in a large non-stick frying pan over a medium heat. Cook for about the same amount of time as listed for grilling.)

Brush the Focaccia slices with the remaining 2 tablespoons olive oil. Toast the Focaccia slices, oil sides down, on the grill or griddle or in a non-stick frying pan until golden brown. Remove the Focaccia from the grill and keep warm or at room temperature while finishing the burgers.

Top the burgers with Fresh Tomato Sauce. Cover with aluminium foil and place in the oven for 10-12 minutes until heated through and cooked. Remove the burgers from the baking tray and the foil. Top each burger with a slice of the mozzarella. Return to the oven for a few moments until the cheese begins to melt.

Serve the burgers on the grilled Focaccia.

Fresh Tomato Sauce

Serves 4

1 tablespoon extra-virgin olive oil
150 g/5 oz onions, finely chopped
1 teaspoon garlic, finely chopped
Salt and pepper
2 tablespoons sweet Marsala wine
2 large tomatoes, peeled, seeded and chopped
2 tablespoons chopped fresh basil
1 tablespoon chopped fresh parsley

Heat the olive oil in a medium non-stick frying pan over a medium-high heat. When hot, add the onions and garlic. Lightly season with salt and pepper and cook for 3-4 minutes. Add the Marsala wine and continue cooking for 2-3 minutes until the Marsala has almost completely evaporated.

Add the tomatoes, lightly season with salt and pepper, reduce the heat to medium and continue cooking about 15 minutes until the sauce thickens. Stir in the basil and parsley. Adjust the seasoning with salt and pepper, then serve.

The sauce can be kept warm in a double boiler for up to 45 minutes before serving. The sauce may also be cooled in an ice-water bath, then stored, tightly covered, in a non-corrosive container for 2 or 3 days. Re-heat the sauce over a medium heat.

 # Shepherd's Pie Burger
with Whipped Potatoes and Country-style Vegetables

Makes 4 burgers

David Burke
Chef/Owner
Park Avenue Cafe
New York, New York

UPON GRADUATION FROM THE CULINARY INSTITUTE OF AMERICA IN 1982, DAVID BURKE CHARTED A PERIPATETIC COURSE THAT LANDED HIM IN SOME OF THE FINEST KITCHENS IN THE UNITED STATES AND EUROPE.

THE RECIPIENT OF NUMEROUS AWARDS AND HONOURS, DAVID WON THE *MEILLEUR OUVRIERS DE FRANCE* DIPLOMA AT THE INTERNATIONAL FOOD FESTIVAL HELD IN TOKYO IN 1988. AT THE SAME COMPETITION, HE WAS PRESENTED WITH THE NIPPON AWARD OF EXCELLENCE BY THE JAPANESE GOVERNMENT.

A SELF-CONFESSED ICONOCLAST, DAVID BURKE ENJOYS EXPERIMENTING WITH DIFFERENT STYLES AND CUISINES. INFLUENCED BY HIS INTERNATIONAL EXPERIENCE, HE HAS DEVELOPED A FLAIR FOR TRANSLATING CLASSIC FOREIGN DISHES INTO UNIQUELY AMERICAN CREATIONS. ONE MIGHT SAY THAT HE HAS INDEED BROKEN NEW GROUND WITH HIS DELECTABLE SHEPHERD'S PIE BURGER.

3 large potatoes, scrubbed but not peeled
625 g/1¼ lb trimmed venison from shoulder or leg, cut into 2.5 cm/1 in pieces (or 625 g/1¼ lb minced trimmed venison from shoulder or leg; see Note)
4 rashers bacon, finely chopped
2 teaspoons freshly ground juniper berries
½ teaspoon salt
½ teaspoon freshly ground black pepper
225 ml/8 fl oz vegetable oil

Trim the ends of the unpeeled potatoes so they are flat. Cut the potatoes, one at a time, into long, thin strands on a Japanese turning slicer (see page 11) fitted with a medium-tooth blade. Immediately place the potato strands in cold water.

If using venison pieces, mince through a meat mincer fitted with a coarse mincing plate into a large stainless steel bowl.

Add the bacon, juniper berries, salt and pepper to the minced venison. Gently but thoroughly combine the ingredients.

Gently form the venison mixture into four 150 g/5 oz burgers, each 2 cm/¾ in thick. Cover the burgers with cling film and refrigerate until needed.

Drain the potatoes. Remove any excess moisture from the potatoes by patting them dry with kitchen towels. Divide the potatoes into 4 equal portions, forming each portion into a small nest. Place a burger in the centre of each nest. Bring the edges of the nest towards the centre to completely enclose the burger (which looks a bit like the top of Medusa's head at this point). Use your hands to slightly press the potatoes into the burger.

Heat half of the vegetable oil in each of 2 large non-stick frying pans over a high heat. When hot, pan-fry the burgers, 2 in each pan, for 6-8 minutes on each side until the potatoes are golden brown. At this point the burgers will be rare to medium-rare; if you desire a more well done burger, place the burgers on a baking tray in a preheated 200°C/400°F/Gas 6 oven for 3-4 minutes for medium and 6-7 minutes for well done.

Place each burger on a dinner plate. Top each with hot Whipped Potatoes and Country-style Vegetables, allowing the vegetables to flow down on to the plate. Serve immediately.

Note: If venison is not part of your larder, substitute beef.

Whipped Potatoes

Serves 4

> **4 potatoes**
> **1 tablespoon salt**
> **225 ml/8 fl oz milk, hot**
> **125 ml/4 fl oz extra-virgin olive oil**
> **Salt and pepper**

Peel the potatoes.

Place the potatoes in a large saucepan with enough water to cover and 1 tablespoon salt. Bring to the boil over a high heat. Lower the heat to medium-high and simmer for 30-35 minutes until the potatoes are cooked through. Drain the water from the potatoes.

Whip the potatoes with the milk and olive oil until smooth in the bowl of an electric mixer fitted with a balloon whip or in a large stainless steel bowl using a wire whisk. Adjust the seasoning with salt and pepper. The potatoes may be served immediately or kept warm in a double boiler for up to 1 hour.

Country-style Vegetables

Serves 4

> **16 pickling onions, peeled**
> **1 carrot, cut in half and thinly sliced diagonally**
> **2 turnips, cut into strips 7.5 cm/3 in long and 0.5 cm/¼ in thick**
> **150 g/5 oz shelled green peas**
> **2 tablespoons extra-virgin olive oil**
> **2 tablespoons water**
> **Salt and pepper**
> **2 tablespoons chopped fresh parsley**

Bring a large saucepan of lightly salted water to the boil. Drop the onions into the boiling water and cook for 2 minutes. Add the carrots and cook for an additional 2 minutes. Add the turnips and cook for 5 minutes. Add the peas and cook for 1 minute. Drain the vegetables, then plunge them into ice water. When the vegetables are cooled, remove from the ice water and drain well.

At this point, the vegetables may be stored, tightly covered, in the refrigerator for up to 2 days.

To serve, heat the olive oil and 2 tablespoons water in a large non-stick frying pan over a medium-high heat. When hot, add the vegetables, lightly season with salt and pepper and cook for 4-5 minutes until hot throughout. Add the parsley and toss to combine. Serve immediately.

Missouri Sirloin and Blue Cheese Burger

with Spiced Tomato Relish and Cornmeal and Black Pepper Bread

Makes 4 burgers

Bill Cardwell
Chef/Owner
Cardwell's
St Louis, Missouri

THE COMBINATION OF FLAVOURS AND TEXTURES THAT CHEF BILL CARDWELL SERVES UP IN HIS MISSOURI BURGER IS JUST THE KIND OF PALATE-INVIGOURATING EXPERIENCE YOU CAN LOOK FORWARD TO AT HIS EPONYMOUS RESTAURANT IN ST LOUIS. SINCE GRADUATING FROM THE CULINARY INSTITUTE OF AMERICA, CHEF CARDWELL HAS MADE A CAREER OF CREATING FOOD WITH BROAD APPEAL. FOR SEVERAL YEARS, HE WAS THE CORPORATE EXECUTIVE CHEF FOR A CONGLOMERATE THAT GAVE AMERICA THE LIKES OF HOULIHAN'S, THE BRISTOL GRILL AND FEDORA. NOW THE ENTERPRISING CHEF CAN BE FOUND DIRECTING HIS OWN FORTUNES, COOKING MEALS THAT HAVE HAD THE FOOD COGNOSCENTI OF ST LOUIS BUZZING SINCE CARDWELL'S OPENED ITS DOORS IN 1986.

---

750 g/1½ lb lean minced sirloin
25 g/1 oz blue cheese
Salt and pepper
50 g/2 oz unsalted butter, softened

4 slices Cheddar cheese, about 25 g/1 oz each
8 rashers smoked bacon, cooked until crisp and drained

Gently form the minced beef into eight 75 g/3 oz patties, each 1 cm/½ in thick.

Use a metal spoon to make a small, shallow indentation in the centre of 4 of the beef patties. Divide the blue cheese into 4 portions, then form each portion into a smooth, round ball. Place a blue cheese ball in each indentation. Top each with another patty and gently form into burgers, making sure to seal all open edges. Season each burger with salt and pepper. Cover the burgers with cling film and refrigerate until needed.

Grill the burgers over a medium wood or charcoal fire. Cook as desired: 4-5 minutes on each side for rare, 6-7 minutes on each side for medium and 9-10 minutes on each side for well done. (This burger may also be cooked on a well-seasoned flat griddle or in a large non-stick frying pan over a medium-high heat. Cook for about the same amount of time as listed for grilling.)

Toast 8 slices of Cornmeal and Black Pepper Bread on the grill or griddle or in a non-stick frying pan for 10-15 seconds on each side.

Serve the burgers on the toasted bread, which has been spread with the softened butter. Top each burger with 1 slice of the Cheddar, 2 slices of the bacon and 1 tablespoon Spiced Tomato Relish. Serve immediately, accompanied by additional Spiced Tomato Relish.

There are several creamy blue vein cheeses available. To add tang to this burger, choose from Danish blue, Roquefort, gorgonzola or blue Stilton.

Spiced Tomato Relish

Makes about 900 g/2 lb

**5 tomatoes, about 900 g/2 lb, peeled, seeded
  and chopped**
200 g/7 oz red onions, very finely chopped
125 ml/4 fl oz red wine vinegar
100 g/3½ oz light brown sugar
175 g/6 oz light corn syrup (see Note)
  6 tablespoons tomato purée
  **1 small hot green or red chilli, very finely
  chopped with seeds**
  1 clove garlic, finely chopped
½ tablespoon finely chopped fresh ginger
  1 teaspoon salt
½ teaspoon ground white pepper
½ teaspoon ground cinnamon
¼ teaspoon ground mace
⅛ teaspoon ground cloves
  1 tablespoon chopped fresh mint

Heat all the ingredients, with the exception of the mint, in a large stainless steel saucepan over a medium-high heat. Bring to the boil, then lower the heat and simmer for 1 hour, stirring frequently. Remove the pan from the heat.

Transfer the relish to a stainless steel bowl. Cool in an ice-water bath until cold. When the relish is cold, add the mint and thoroughly combine.

Refrigerate the relish in a stainless steel or another non-corrosive container for at least 24 hours before serving.

The quantity of relish produced by this recipe is more than enough to accompany the sirloin burgers. Any remaining relish will keep, tightly covered, in the refrigerator for several days.

Note: Light corn syrup is a popular American ingredient refined from the sugar in sweet corn. It is less sweet than sugar. It is sometimes sold in gourmet food shops but if it is unavailable, substitute golden syrup. If you use golden syrup, however, add the sugar to taste after you have combined all the other ingredients.

This relish is not only an excellent burger condiment, it also enhances such grilled meats as pork and chicken.

Cornmeal and Black Pepper Bread

Makes 1 loaf (sixteen 1 cm/½ in slices)

2 tablespoons clear honey
2 teaspoons dried yeast
50 ml/2 fl oz water, hot (about 50°C/120°F)
325 g/11 oz plain flour
150 ml/5 fl oz buttermilk, plus 2 tablespoons
65 g/2½ oz yellow cornmeal, plus 1 teaspoon
1 tablespoon vegetable oil, plus 1 teaspoon
2 teaspoons salt
2 teaspoons freshly cracked black pepper
1 egg yolk, size 3

In the bowl of an electric mixer, place the honey and yeast in the hot water and stir gently to dissolve. Allow the mixture to stand and foam for 10 minutes.

Place the mixing bowl on an electric mixer fitted with a dough hook. On top of the honey-yeast mixture, add all but 25 g/1 oz of the flour, 150 ml/5 fl oz buttermilk, 65 g/2½ oz cornmeal, 1 tablespoon vegetable oil, salt and pepper. Mix on a medium speed for 2 minutes, then scrape down the sides of the bowl. Continue to mix on a medium speed for 3-3½ minutes until the dough forms a ball. (If a table-model electric mixer is not available, follow the directions using a hand-held mixer or kneading by hand. The mixing times will increase depending upon which alternative method is used.)

Coat the inside of a stainless steel bowl with the remaining vegetable oil. Place the dough in the bowl and wipe the bowl with the dough. Cover the bowl with cling film. Allow the dough to rise in a warm location for 1½ hours or until it has doubled in volume.

Flatten the dough into a 20 × 25 cm/8 × 10 in rectangle on a clean, lightly floured work surface, using the remaining flour as necessary. Tightly roll the flattened dough into a 25 cm/10 in long loaf. Transfer the loaf to a baking tray that has been sprinkled with the remaining teaspoon cornmeal. Loosely cover the loaf with cling film. Allow the loaf to rise in a warm location for 45 minutes or until doubled in size.

Preheat the oven to 180°C/350°F/Gas 4.

Whisk the remaining 2 tablespoons buttermilk with the egg yolk, then lightly brush the top of the loaf with this egg wash. Use a sharp knife or a razor blade to make 3 diagonal, evenly spaced 0.5 cm/¼ in deep cuts on the surface of the loaf.

Bake the loaf for 30-35 minutes. To test if it is baked, lightly tap the base of the baked loaf; a hollow sound will indicate that the bread is done. Remove the baked loaf from the baking tray and allow to cool to room temperature before slicing.

> *There is something very Italianate about this bread; both the taste and texture remind one of polenta. Try basting the sliced bread with olive oil and fresh chopped herbs, then grilling over a wood fire. The smell and taste may well suggest that you have arrived in Apulia!*

Vegetable Pan Burger
with Roasted Garlic Paste

Makes 4 burgers

Michael Chiarello

Chef/Owner
Tra Vigne
St Helena, California

GROWING UP IN A HOME WHERE EVERY-
THING CENTRED ROUND THE TABLE AND
THE GARDEN NATURALLY ATTRACTED
MICHAEL CHIARELLO TO A CAREER IN
COOKING. MANY OF HIS FAMILY MEMBERS
MADE A LIVING AS BUTCHERS OR
RANCHERS, AND MICHAEL FOLLOWED SUIT
BY WORKING IN RESTAURANTS FROM THE
AGE OF FOURTEEN AND THEN ATTENDING
AND GRADUATING FROM THE CULINARY
INSTITUTE OF AMERICA.

SINCE 1987, MICHAEL HAS BEEN THE CHEF/
OWNER OF THE CRITICALLY ACCLAIMED
TRA VIGNE IN ST HELENA, CALIFORNIA.

AT TRA VIGNE, MICHAEL AND HIS YOUNG
CREW PRODUCE THEIR OWN ITALIAN-
INSPIRED DISHES FEATURING SUCH
INGREDIENTS AS PROSCIUTTO, BRESAOLA,
SALAMI AND CURED OLIVES. AND IN
ADDITION TO OPERATING THE VERY BUSY
RESTAURANT, THERE IS A GARDEN TO TEND
AND OLIVE OIL TO PRODUCE.

MICHAEL'S BURGER WAS INSPIRED BY
A SOUTHERN ITALIAN DISH HIS FAMILY
OFTEN ENJOYED.

4 tablespoons extra-virgin olive oil

1 leek, white part only, cut into thin strips 6 cm/2½ in long

1 teaspoon finely chopped garlic

225 g/8 oz fresh wild mushrooms, stalks trimmed or removed as necessary and sliced (see Note)

Salt and freshly ground black pepper

1 tomato, peeled, seeded and chopped

150 g/5 oz shelled green peas, blanched

1 red pepper, roasted, skinned, seeded and cut into thin strips

6 spinach leaves, stalks removed, washed, dried and cut into thin strips

2 tablespoons coarsely chopped fresh basil

1 teaspoon chopped fresh thyme

50 g/2 oz dry breadcrumbs

50 g/2 oz Parmesan cheese, freshly grated

4 slices Focaccia (see page 82)

4 slices fontina cheese, about 25 g/1 oz each (see Note)

Heat the olive oil in a large non-stick frying pan over a medium heat. When hot, add the leek and garlic and cook for 1 minute. Increase the heat to medium-high, then add the wild mushrooms and lightly season with salt and pepper. Cook for 4-5 minutes. Add the tomato, lightly season with salt and pepper and continue cooking about 2 minutes until most of the liquid has evaporated. Add the peas, red pepper, spinach, basil and thyme. Stir constantly for 2 minutes until heated through. Transfer the vegetables to a large stainless steel bowl, then stir in the breadcrumbs and Parmesan. Adjust the seasoning with salt and pepper. Allow the mixture to cool to room temperature.

Preheat the oven to 190°C/375°F/Gas 5.

Gently form the mixture into four 175 g/6 oz burgers, each 2.5 cm/1 in thick. Cover the burgers with cling film and refrigerate until needed.

41

Toast the Focaccia slices in the oven for 2 minutes. Spread the cut side of the Focaccia slices with Roasted Garlic Paste. Place a vegetable burger on each slice of Focaccia. Place the burgers on a baking tray and top each burger with a slice of the fontina. Bake for 16–18 minutes until the cheese melts and begins to brown and the burgers are heated through. Remove the burgers and Focaccia from the oven and serve immediately.

Note: If fresh wild mushrooms are not available, an excellent substitution is fresh shiitake mushrooms. Although these mushrooms are cultivated, they have a wonderful earthy flavour. Sixty grams/2 oz dried shiitake mushrooms rehydrated in warm water for 1 hour can also be used. Drain thoroughly before using.

Fontina is an Italian cheese with a supple texture. You can use Port-Salut or havarti instead.

Roasted Garlic Paste

Serves 4

1 large head garlic
  Salt and pepper
2 sprigs fresh thyme
2 tablespoons extra-virgin olive oil

Preheat the oven to 160°C/325°F/Gas 3.

Cut 1 cm/½ in off the top of the head of garlic, exposing the cloves. Place the head in a small ovenproof dish and lightly season with salt and pepper. Top the head with the sprigs of fresh thyme and drizzle with the olive oil. Cover the dish tightly with aluminium foil, then bake for about 40 minutes until they are very tender. Remove the garlic from the oven and allow to cool, uncovered, in the olive oil for at least 1 hour at room temperature.

When cool, gently separate the cloves. Squeeze the garlic pulp out of the cloves into a small, non-corrosive bowl. Use a fork to mash the garlic pulp into a rough, textured paste. Use immediately or keep tightly covered in the refrigerator for up to several days.

Solon Burger
with Fresh Herb Cheese and Vegetable Coleslaw

Makes 4 burgers

Richard Czack
Executive Assistant to the Vice President of Education
The Culinary Institute of America
Hyde Park, New York

BEGINNING WITH HIS EXPERIENCE IN A BAKERY IN HIS HOMETOWN OF CLEVELAND, RICHARD CZACK HAS MADE A CAREER OF STRIVING FOR EXCELLENCE. HE BUILT HIS SKILLS IN THE MILITARY AND THEN AS A STUDENT AT THE CULINARY INSTITUTE OF AMERICA, WHERE HE GRADUATED WITH TOP HONOURS.

RICHARD'S INVOLVEMENT WITH THE INSTITUTE AND HIS ACCRUEMENT OF HONOURS HAVE CONTINUED. HE JOINED THE INSTITUTE'S FACULTY IN 1970 AND, AFTER YEARS OF BEING A CHEF-INSTRUCTOR, HE NOW SERVES AS EXECUTIVE ASSISTANT TO THE VICE PRESIDENT OF EDUCATION. IN 1988, RICHARD WAS CERTIFIED A MASTER CHEF, ONE OF FEWER THAN ONE HUNDRED IN THE UNITED STATES.

RICHARD HAS NOT FORGOTTEN HIS OHIO ROOTS, AND HIS SOLON BURGER IS NAMED FOR A CITY THAT HE USED TO CALL HOME IN THAT MID-WESTERN STATE.

1 tablespoon olive oil
2 tablespoons finely chopped onions
450 g/1 lb minced sirloin
225 g/8 oz minced veal
Salt and white pepper
4 Best Burger Buns (see page 109), cut in half

Heat the olive oil in a small frying pan over a medium heat. When hot, add the onions and cook lightly for 3 minutes or until translucent. Transfer the onions to a plate and place, uncovered, in the refrigerator to cool.

In a large stainless steel bowl, gently but thoroughly combine the chilled onions with the minced beef and minced veal. Season with salt and pepper.

Gently form the meat mixture into four 175 g/6 oz burgers, each 2.5 cm/ 1 in thick. Cover the burgers with cling film and refrigerate until needed.

Grill the burgers over a medium wood or charcoal fire. Cook as desired: 5 minutes on each side for medium-rare, 6-7 minutes on each side for medium and 8-9 minutes on each side for well done. (This burger may also be cooked on a well-seasoned flat griddle or in a large non-stick frying pan over a medium-high heat. Cook for about the same amount of time as listed for grilling.)

Remove the burgers from the grill and top each with a slice of Fresh Herb Cheese.

Toast the buns, cut sides down, on the grill or griddle or in a non-stick frying pan until golden brown. Serve the burgers on the toasted buns accompanied by Chef Czack's vivid and crunchy Vegetable Coleslaw.

Fresh Herb Cheese

Serves 4

125 g/4 oz full-fat soft cheese, softened
1 tablespoon soured cream
½ teaspoon finely chopped fresh chervil
½ teaspoon finely chopped fresh chives
½ teaspoon finely chopped fresh dill
½ teaspoon finely chopped fresh parsley
½ teaspoon finely chopped fresh thyme

Place the softened cheese in a stainless steel bowl and add the remaining ingredients. Blend the ingredients until smooth.

Place the cheese on cling film or greaseproof paper and roll into a solid, uniformly round tube shape approximately 4.5 cm/1³/4 in in diameter.

Place the herb cheese in the freezer for about 1 hour until firm but not frozen solid. Remove the wrapping and cut the cheese into 4 slices. Cover and refrigerate until needed.

Vegetable Coleslaw

Serves 4

4 tablespoons white wine vinegar
2 tablespoons sugar
4 tablespoons vegetable oil
Salt and pepper
75 g/3 oz red cabbage, shredded
75 g/3 oz white cabbage, shredded
65 g/2½ oz carrots, julienned
65 g/2½ oz green peppers, julienned
65 g/2½ oz red peppers, julienned
65 g/2½ oz red onions, thinly sliced
2 spring onions, trimmed and thinly sliced
1 tablespoon finely chopped fresh chives
1 tablespoon chopped fresh parsley
½ teaspoon celery seeds

In a large stainless steel bowl, whisk together the white wine vinegar and sugar. Continue to whisk until the sugar is dissolved. Then whisk in a slow, steady stream of the vegetable oil. Adjust the seasoning with salt and pepper and combine thoroughly. Add the remaining ingredients and toss gently to combine. Cover the bowl with cling film and refrigerate for 2 hours before serving. The coleslaw may be kept refrigerated for 2 or 3 days.

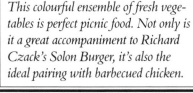

This colourful ensemble of fresh vegetables is perfect picnic food. Not only is it a great accompaniment to Richard Czack's Solon Burger, it's also the ideal pairing with barbecued chicken.

Blues Burger

with Quick Barbecue Sauce, Sautéed Mushrooms and Cheese Fries

Makes 4 burgers

Edward Daggers
Executive Chef
Kingsmill Resort
Williamsburg, Virginia

WORKING IN FOUR- AND FIVE-STAR RESORTS HAS NOT MADE EDWARD DAGGERS FORGET THE AMERICAN LOVE AFFAIR WITH BURGERS. ED HAS WON SEVERAL AWARDS IN CULINARY SHOWS, AND HIS ABILITIES IN ICE CARVING AND FOOD DECORATION HAVE GAINED HIM REGIONAL RENOWN. BUT WHEN IT GETS RIGHT DOWN TO THE BASICS, AND WHEN YOU ARE THE CHEF AT THE RESORT THAT HOSTS THE ANHEUSER-BUSCH GOLF CLASSIC, YOUR SKILLS MUST INCLUDE THE ABILITY TO PREPARE WITH ENTHUSIASM AND CREATIVITY FOODS SUCH AS HAMBURGERS.

ED DAGGERS' RECIPE IS SURE TO HAVE YOU FANTASIZING ABOUT BURGERS.

750 g/1½ lb minced sirloin
½ teaspoon ground cumin
½ teaspoon paprika
¼ teaspoon freshly ground black pepper
¼ teaspoon chilli powder
¼ teaspoon salt

Pinch cayenne pepper
50 g/2 oz of your favourite blue cheese
Salt and pepper
4 Onion Rolls (see page 89), cut in half

In a large stainless steel bowl, gently but thoroughly combine the minced beef, cumin, paprika, freshly ground black pepper, chilli powder, ¼ teaspoon salt and cayenne pepper.

Gently form the seasoned beef into eight 75 g/3 oz patties, each 1 cm/½ in thick. Use a metal spoon to make a small, shallow indentation in the centre of 4 of the patties. Place 15 g/½ oz blue cheese into each indentation, then top each with another patty and gently form into 3 cm/1¼ in thick burgers, making sure to seal all open edges. Cover the burgers with cling film and refrigerate until needed.

Just before grilling, lightly season the burgers with salt and pepper, then coat with Quick Barbecue Sauce. Grill the burgers over a medium wood or charcoal fire. Cook as desired: 4-5 minutes on each side for rare, 6-7 minutes on each side for medium and 9-10 minutes on each side for well done. Frequently baste the burgers during the grilling with Quick Barbecue Sauce. (This burger may also be cooked on a well-seasoned flat griddle or in a large non-stick frying pan over a medium-high heat. Cook for about the same amount of time as listed for grilling.)

Remove the burgers from the grill and baste with the remaining Quick Barbecue Sauce. Toast the rolls, cut sides down, on the grill or griddle or in a non-stick frying pan until golden brown. Place each burger on the bottom half of a toasted roll and top with Sautéed Mushrooms and the other half of the roll. Serve the burgers immediately with Cheese Fries.

Quick Barbecue Sauce

Makes about 150 ml/5 fl oz

4 tablespoons ketchup
4 tablespoons light brown sugar
2 tablespoons spicy brown mustard
2 tablespoons dark molasses or treacle
2 tablespoons cider vinegar
2 cloves garlic, peeled and crushed

Heat all the ingredients in a large saucepan over a medium-high heat. Bring the mixture to the boil, then adjust the heat and allow to simmer for 30 minutes, stirring frequently. Remove the pan from the heat, then remove and discard the garlic cloves. The sauce may be used immediately or cooled in an ice-water bath. It will keep tightly covered in the refrigerator for several days. Warm the sauce before using.

Sautéed Mushrooms

Serves 4

25 g/1 oz unsalted butter
2 tablespoons finely chopped onion
2 tablespoons finely chopped spring onion
225 g/8 oz fresh mushrooms, sliced
Salt and pepper
2 tablespoons beer

Melt the butter in a medium non-stick frying pan over a medium-high heat. When the butter has melted, add the onions and spring onions and cook for 2-3 minutes until they are tender. Add the mushrooms and season with salt and pepper, then cook 3-4 minutes until most of the moisture has evaporated.

Add the beer to the mixture, then add salt and pepper to taste.

The mushrooms may be used immediately or cooled and re-heated when needed.

Cheese Fries

Serves 4

3 large potatoes, washed and scrubbed clean
225 ml/8 fl oz vegetable oil
Salt and pepper
4 tablespoons beer
225 g/8 oz Cheddar cheese, grated
1 teaspoon Tabasco Sauce
4 rashers bacon, cooked until crisp and crumbled

Use a sharp knife to cut the potatoes into 0.5 cm/¼ in thick slices. Cut the slices into 0.5 cm/¼ in thick strips. The potatoes may be fried immediately or covered with cold water and refrigerated for several hours.

Preheat the oven to 120°C/250°F/Gas ½.

Heat the vegetable oil in a large heavy-based frying pan over a high heat to a temperature of 190°C/375°F. While the oil is heating, drain and thoroughly dry the potatoes on kitchen paper.

Fry the potatoes in the hot oil, one-half at a time, for 6-7 minutes until crispy and golden brown. Drain on kitchen paper and season with salt and pepper. Keep the potatoes warm in the preheated oven while preparing the cheese.

Heat 2.5 cm/1 in water in the bottom half of a double boiler over a low heat. Heat the beer in the top half of the double boiler. When hot, add the Cheddar. Constantly stir the cheese for 4 minutes until smooth. Add the Tabasco Sauce and stir to combine.

Remove the potatoes from the oven and place on a serving plate. Pour over the cheese, then garnish with the bacon. Serve immediately.

The fries may be kept in the preheated oven for up to 30 minutes. However, the cheese should be prepared just moments before serving.

Sicilian Burger

with Semolina Olive Buns and Marinated
Cauliflower Salad

Makes 4 burgers

Sanford D'Amato
Chef/Owner
Sanford Restaurant
Milwaukee, Wisconsin

SOME MIGHT SAY THAT SANFORD D'AMATO
WALKED IMMEDIATELY INTO THE
LIMELIGHT. THE TRUTH IS THAT SANFORD
TOILED MANY YEARS IN A VARIETY OF
FOOD-SERVICE OPERATIONS, BEGINNING
IN HIS TEENS IN MILWAUKEE-AREA
RESTAURANTS. AFTER GRADUATING FROM
THE CULINARY INSTITUTE OF AMERICA,
HE COOKED AND HONED HIS CRAFT IN
RESTAURANTS IN NEW YORK CITY BEFORE
RETURNING TO MILWAUKEE, WHERE
HE DREAMED OF OPENING HIS OWN
RESTAURANT. HE ACCOMPLISHED THAT
GOAL IN 1989, WHEN HE AND HIS WIFE,
ANGELA, OPENED SANFORD RESTAURANT
IN A BUILDING THAT AT ONE TIME HOUSED
HIS GRANDFATHER'S GROCERY STORE.

SINCE THAT DAY, SANFORD'S RESTAURANT
HAS ACHIEVED MUCH NATIONAL
RECOGNITION, INCLUDING A LISTING
IN *ESQUIRE* MAGAZINE AS ONE OF THE
NATION'S BEST NEW RESTAURANTS.

SANFORD'S SICILIAN BURGER WAS
INSPIRED BY THE BURGERS HIS GRAND-
FATHER MADE FOR HIM AT THE GROCERY
STORE WHERE HE HAD WORKED AS A
YOUNGSTER.

4 tablespoons extra-virgin
    olive oil
65 g/2½ oz onion, finely
    chopped
4 tablespoons dry white wine
2 tablespoons sweet Marsala
    wine
1 small bay leaf
1 teaspoon freshly ground
    black pepper
½ teaspoon salt
450 g/1 lb minced beef
225 g/8 oz minced pork

1 egg, size 3, lightly beaten
25 g/1 oz dry white
    breadcrumbs
25 g/1 oz Romano cheese,
    grated
2 tablespoons chopped fresh
    parsley
1 tablespoon chopped fresh
    basil
Salt and freshly ground
    black pepper

Heat 2 tablespoons olive oil in a small non-stick frying pan over a medium-high heat. When hot, add the onions and cook for 3-4 minutes until translucent. Add the white wine, Marsala wine, bay leaf, 1 teaspoon freshly ground black pepper and ½ teaspoon salt. Bring the mixture to the boil, then adjust the heat and allow to simmer for 9-10 minutes until most of the liquid has evaporated. Discard the bay leaf. Transfer the onion mixture to a plate and place, uncovered, in the refrigerator to cool.

In a large stainless steel bowl, gently but thoroughly combine the minced beef, minced pork, chilled onion mixture, egg, breadcrumbs, Romano, parsley and basil.

Gently form the seasoned meat mixture into four 225 g/8 oz burgers, each 3 cm/1¼ in thick. Cover the burgers with cling film and refrigerate until needed.

Just before grilling, lightly season the burgers with salt and freshly ground black pepper. Grill the burgers over a medium wood or charcoal fire. Cook as desired: 6-7 minutes on each side for medium and 9-10 minutes on each side for medium-well. (This burger may also be cooked on a well-seasoned flat griddle or in a large non-stick frying pan over a medium-high heat. Cook for about the same amount of time as listed for grilling.)

49

Remove the burgers from the grill. Cut 4 Semolina Olive Buns in half. Lightly brush the bun halves with the remaining olive oil. Toast the buns, oiled sides down, on the grill or griddle or in a non-stick frying pan until golden. Serve the Sicilian Burgers on the toasted buns, accompanied by the Marinated Cauliflower Salad.

Semolina Olive Buns

Makes 8 buns

350 ml/12 fl oz warm water
2 tablespoons extra-virgin olive oil, plus 1 teaspoon
1 tablespoon barley malt (see Note)
1 teaspoon sugar
2 tablespoons dried yeast
350 g/12 oz plain flour
175 g/6 oz semolina flour (see Note)
2 teaspoons salt
65 g/2½ oz oil-cured, ripe black olives, stoned and chopped

In the bowl of an electric mixer, place the warm water, 1 tablespoon olive oil, barley malt and sugar and stir gently to dissolve the sugar. Add the yeast and stir to dissolve. Allow the mixture to stand and foam for 5 minutes.

Place the mixing bowl with the yeast mixture on an electric mixer fitted with a dough hook. Add 300 g/10 oz of the plain flour, the semolina flour and salt and mix on a low speed for 1 minute. Stop the mixer and scrape down the bowl. Continue mixing on a medium–low speed for 5-6 minutes until the dough is very smooth and elastic. (If a table-model electric mixer is not available, follow the directions using a hand-held mixer or kneading by hand. The mixing times will increase depending upon which alternative method is used.)

Place the dough on a clean, lightly floured work surface, using the remaining plain flour as necessary. Flatten the dough. Place the olives on top, then fold the dough from end to end and knead the olives into the dough for 2-3 minutes.

Coat the inside of a stainless steel bowl with 1 teaspoon olive oil. Place the dough in the bowl and wipe the bowl with the dough. Cover the bowl with cling film. Allow the dough to rise in a warm location about 1 hour until it has doubled in size.

Preheat the oven to 160°C/325°F/Gas 3.

Place the dough on a lightly floured work surface. Use a sharp knife to cut the dough into 8 equal portions. Shape each portion into a ball. Place the balls on a baking tray lined with baking parchment. Loosely cover the dough with cling film and allow to rise in a warm location about 30 minutes until doubled in size.

Using a dough cutter or the back side of a thin-bladed knife, press an X on the top of each bun (be sure not to cut the buns). Allow the buns to rise for an additional 10 minutes. Brush with the remaining tablespoon olive oil.

Bake the buns for 35-40 minutes until golden brown.

Allow the buns to cool thoroughly before cutting in half.

The buns will keep fresh for 2 or 3 days stored in a sealed polythene bag at room temperature.

Note: Look for barley malt and semolina flour in health food shops, or in the health-food section at your supermarket.

Marinated Cauliflower Salad

Serves 4

450 ml/³⁄₄ pint water
225 ml/8 fl oz red wine vinegar
65 g/2¹⁄₂ oz sugar
4 cloves garlic, peeled
2 small bay leaves
2 small sprigs fresh thyme
1 small sprig fresh rosemary
3 whole allspice berries, crushed
2 whole cloves
1 tablespoon cracked black pepper
¹⁄₂ teaspoon salt
300 g/10 oz caulifower, broken into small florets
150 g/5 oz carrots, thinly sliced
65 g/2¹⁄₂ oz red onions, chopped
65 g/2¹⁄₂ oz red pepper, julienned
150 g/5 oz green brine-cured olives, sliced
50 g/2 oz peperoncini (see Note), seeded and sliced
2 teaspoons capers, rinsed and chopped
225 ml/8 fl oz extra-virgin olive oil
25 g/1 oz basil leaves, thinly sliced
Salt and freshly ground black pepper

To prepare the marinade, heat the water, red wine vinegar, sugar, garlic, bay leaves, thyme, rosemary, allspice, cloves, cracked black pepper and salt in a large stainless steel or other non-corrosive saucepan over a high heat. Bring the mixture to the boil. Remove the pan from the heat, cover and allow to stand for 30 minutes. Strain (and reserve) the marinade through a fine mesh sieve or several folds of muslin.

Return the marinade to the saucepan, then add the cauliflower, carrots, onions and red pepper and return the saucepan to a high heat. As soon as the mixture boils, remove the pan from the heat. Add the olives, peperoncini and capers. Allow to cool at room temperature. When cool, cover and refrigerate about 1 hour until thoroughly chilled. Drain the vegetables in a colander.

In a stainless steel or other non-metallic bowl, toss the vegetables with the olive oil and basil. Season to taste with salt and freshly ground black pepper, then serve immediately.

This salad will keep tightly covered in the refrigerator for several days.

Note: Peperoncini are small hot and sweet peppers sold in their pickling juice. They are available in Italian delicatessens or gourmet food shops.

> *Food-related childhood memories abound for Sanford. A common sight in his family's grocery store was the large glass jars containing a colourful mix of pickled vegetables known as* giardiniera. *If only Grandfather could taste this salad!*

////////////////// Shiitake Mushroom Burger \\\\\\\\\\\\\\\\\\

with Black-eye Bean and Roasted Pepper Salad and
Crispy Potato Cakes

Makes 8 burgers

Marcel Desaulniers
Chef/Co-Owner
The Trellis Restaurant
Williamsburg, Virginia

AFTER MARCEL DESAULNIERS GRADUATED AT THE AGE OF NINETEEN FROM THE CULINARY INSTITUTE, HE WENT TO THE BIG APPLE TO HONE HIS CRAFT. FOLLOWING A YEAR OF COOKING AT PRIVATE CLUBS IN NEW YORK, HE WAS ASKED TO HONE A CRAFT OF A DIFFERENT KIND WHEN HE WAS DRAFTED INTO THE U.S. MARINE CORPS. FOLLOWING A TOUR OF DUTY IN VIETNAM, WHERE HIS ONLY MEALS WERE C RATIONS, MARCEL RETURNED TO NEW YORK CITY TO WORK AT THE PIERRE HOTEL. IN 1970, HE WENT TO VIRGINIA TO WORK FOR THE COLONIAL WILLIAMSBURG FOUNDATION'S RESTAURANT OPERATIONS.

IN WILLIAMSBURG, MARCEL OBSERVED, RELISHED AND INSPIRED THE REBIRTH OF AMERICAN CUISINE. HE OPENED THE TRELLIS RESTAURANT IN 1980 AND HAS RECEIVED ACCOLADES EVER SINCE.

SOME SAY MARCEL IS A CULINARY PARADOX, HAVING AUTHORED THE WILDLY POPULAR *DEATH BY CHOCOLATE* WHILE PRACTISING A NEARLY MONASTICAL REGIME OF HEALTHY EATING. HIS THEORY IS THAT FOOD CAN BE BOTH HEALTHY AND DELICIOUS...BUT AN OCCASIONAL INDULGENCE IS GOOD FOR THE SOUL.

HIS BURGER IS AN EXAMPLE OF HEALTHY EATING THAT HAS ALL THE QUALITIES OF SERIOUS INDULGENCE.

175 g/6 oz dried black-eye beans, washed and picked over
1 large potato
3 tablespoons extra-virgin olive oil
2 spring onions, very finely chopped

900 g/2 lb fresh shiitake mushrooms, stalks removed and thinly sliced (see Note)
Salt and pepper
2 tablespoons chopped fresh parsley
2 teaspoons chopped fresh thyme

Soak the black-eye beans overnight in cold water to cover.

Drain and rinse the soaked beans. Place in a large saucepan and cover with lightly salted water. Bring to the boil over a high heat, then adjust the heat and allow the beans to simmer for about 35 minutes until very tender. Drain the beans. Transfer to a plate and place, uncovered, in the refrigerator to cool.

In a large saucepan, cover the potato with cold water. Bring to the boil over a high heat, then adjust the heat and allow the potato to simmer for 35-40 minutes until cooked through. Transfer to a plate and place, uncovered, in the refrigerator to cool.

Heat 2 tablespoons olive oil in a large non-stick frying pan over a medium heat. When hot, add the spring onions and cook for 1 minute. Add the shiitake mushrooms, then season with salt and pepper. Adjust the heat to medium-high and cook for 7-8 minutes until very tender. Transfer to a plate and place, uncovered, in the refrigerator to cool.

Peel and grate the thoroughly cooled potato. Combine 225 g/8 oz of the grated potato (the whole peeled potato may yield slightly more; use only the specified amount) with the cooked black-eye beans, sautéed shiitake mushrooms, parsley and thyme in a stainless steel bowl. Season with salt and pepper. Mix well using your hands (be certain to thoroughly combine the ingredients, squashing some of the beans while mixing).

Gently form the mushroom mixture into eight 175 g/6 oz burgers, each 3 cm/1¼ in thick. Cover the burgers with cling film and refrigerate until needed.

Preheat the oven to 180°C/350°F/Gas 4.

Heat a large non-stick frying pan that has been lightly brushed with the remaining 1 tablespoon olive oil over a medium-high heat. Sear 4 of the burgers in the hot pan for 2 minutes on each side until crispy and golden brown. Transfer the burgers to a baking tray. Repeat the procedure with the remaining 4 burgers, then place on the baking tray with the other burgers and bake for 12-14 minutes until heated through.

Portion Black-eye Bean and Roasted Pepper Salad onto 8 dinner plates. Place Crispy Potato Cakes in the centre of the salads, then set the burgers on the potato cakes. Serve immediately.

Note: Until just a few years ago, shiitake mushrooms were marketed primarily in the dried form. Today, one can find fresh shiitake mushrooms in almost any good supermarket's produce department. A cooked shiitake tastes at once silky and smooth, and as it is chewed, it has a nutty, almost meatlike impression.

Shiitake mushrooms are available virtually year-round. They can be stored in the refrigerator for 2-4 weeks, depending upon the moisture content when they are harvested. They will, however, lose some of their woody aroma the longer they are stored.

Black-eye Bean and Roasted Pepper Salad

Serves 8

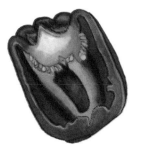

40 g/1½ oz dried black-eye beans, washed and picked over (see Note)

225 ml/8 fl oz extra-virgin olive oil

4 tablespoons balsamic vinegar

2 tablespoons whole-grain mustard

1 teaspoon salt

1 teaspoon cracked black pepper

2 large red peppers, roasted, skinned, seeded and cut into 0.5 cm/¼ in pieces

2 heads lollo biondo lettuce, cut into bite-size pieces, washed and dried

54

Soak the black-eye beans overnight in cold water to cover.

Drain and rinse the soaked beans. Place in a large saucepan and cover with lightly salted water. Bring to the boil over a high heat, then adjust the heat and simmer the beans about 35 minutes until very tender. Drain the beans, transfer to a plate and place, uncovered, in the refrigerator to cool.

In a large stainless steel bowl, whisk together the olive oil, balsamic vinegar, mustard, salt and pepper. Add the cooled black-eye beans and red pepper pieces and combine thoroughly. Add the lettuce pieces and toss to coat the greens. Serve immediately. The salad may be stored tightly covered in the refrigerator for several hours.

Note: Although I call for dried black-eye beans in this recipe, you may certainly substitute fresh beans or peas when available (primarily during the summer months). If you are using fresh peas, skip the soaking step and boil them until tender.

Crispy Potato Cakes

Makes 8 potato cakes

4 large potatoes
1 egg, size 3, lightly beaten
   Salt and pepper
2 tablespoons olive oil

In a large saucepan, cover 1 of the potatoes with cold water, then bring to the boil over a high heat. Adjust the heat and simmer the potato for 35-40 minutes until cooked through. Transfer to a plate and place, uncovered, in the refrigerator for about 1 hour to cool.

Peel and grate the thoroughly cooled potato into a stainless steel bowl. Add 2 tablespoons beaten egg (an average size 3 egg will yield about 4 tablespoons), season with salt and pepper and stir well to combine. Store in the refrigerator until needed.

Bring a large saucepan of lightly salted water to the boil.

While the water is heating, thoroughly wash the remaining 3 potatoes (do not peel). Trim the ends of the potatoes so that they are flat. Cut the potatoes, one at a time, into long, thin strands on a Japanese turning slicer (see page 11) fitted with a medium-tooth blade. Place the potato strands in cold water immediately.

Drain the potato strands in a colander. Lightly blanch the potatoes by placing them into the boiling water for 60 seconds. Drain the blanched potatoes and place them on a baking sheet that has been lined with kitchen paper. Place, uncovered, in the refrigerator to cool. When thoroughly cool, remove any excess moisture from the potatoes by patting them dry with kitchen paper.

Gently but thoroughly combine the potato-egg mixture with the blanched potato strands. Form the potatoes into eight 75 g/3 oz cakes, each 1 cm/½ in thick. The cakes may be cooked immediately or covered with cling film and stored in the refrigerator for up to 24 hours.

Preheat the oven to 110°C/225°F/Gas ½.

Heat a large non-stick frying pan that has been lightly brushed with the olive oil over a high heat. Season the cakes with salt and pepper. When the pan is hot, pan-fry the cakes, 4 at a time, for 9-10 minutes on each side until golden brown and crispy. Keep the cakes warm in the oven while repeating the cooking procedure with the remaining 4 cakes (or if you have 2 large non-stick pans, do all 8 cakes simultaneously). Serve immediately.

The cakes may be kept in the oven for up to 45 minutes after being pan-fried.

Low-Country Rabbit Burger

with Carrot Wheat Bread, Pecan Butter and Celery and Chicory Salad

Makes 4 burgers

Robert Dickson
Chef/Owner
Robert's of Charleston
Charleston, South Carolina

ROBERT DICKSON IS AN IMPRESARIO OF DISTINCTIVE MAGNITUDE. CHEF/OWNER OF HIS INTERNATIONALLY ACCLAIMED EPONYMOUS RESTAURANT, ROBERT IS AT CENTRE STAGE EVERY EVENING, ENJOYING HIS ROLE AS CHEF, RESTAURATEUR AND ACCOMPLISHED OPERA SINGER.

FOLLOWING HIS GRADUATION FROM THE INSTITUTE IN 1963, ROBERT COOKED FOR AND WITH SOME OF THE NOTABLES OF THE FOOD WORLD, NOT THE LEAST BEING JULIA CHILD. HOWEVER, ROBERT'S LOVE AND TALENT FOR OPERA LED HIM TO LONDON, WHERE HE STUDIED OPERA FOR SEVERAL YEARS. NOT WISHING TO BECOME AN EXPATRIATE, ROBERT RETURNED STATESIDE IN 1976 TO COMBINE HIS TWO LOVES AT ROBERT'S OF CHARLESTON. THE REST, AS THEY SAY, IS HISTORY.

THE ALMOST MELODIC INTONATIONS OF ROBERT'S LOW-COUNTRY RABBIT BURGER AND ITS ACCOMPANIMENTS ARE INDICATIVE OF THIS GENTLE MAN'S NATURE.

25 g/1 oz Carrot Wheat Bread breadcrumbs
50 ml/2 fl oz cold chicken stock
450 g/1 lb boned and trimmed rabbit meat from loin sections, cut into 2.5 cm/ 1 in pieces (or 450 g/1 lb minced rabbit meat; see Note)
50 g/2 oz salt-cured ham, finely chopped
65 g/2½ oz onion, finely chopped
2 tablespoons very finely chopped spring onions
1 teaspoon chopped fresh thyme
½ teaspoon cracked black pepper
½ teaspoon celery salt
Salt and freshly ground black pepper

In a small stainless steel bowl, combine the breadcrumbs and cold chicken stock. Cover with cling film and refrigerate until needed.

If using rabbit pieces, mince through a meat mincer fitted with a coarse mincing plate into a large stainless steel bowl.

Gently but thoroughly combine the minced rabbit with the ham, chilled breadcrumb mixture, onions, spring onions, thyme, cracked black pepper and celery salt.

Gently form the seasoned rabbit into four 175 g/6 oz burgers, each 2.5 cm/ 1 in thick. Cover the burgers with cling film and refrigerate until needed.

Preheat the oven to 180°C/350°F/Gas 4.

Just before cooking the burgers, lightly season them with salt and freshly ground black pepper. Heat a large non-stick frying pan over a medium-high heat. When hot, pan-sear the burgers for 5-6 minutes on each side until golden brown. Transfer the rabbit burgers to a baking tray and finish cooking in the oven for 4-5 minutes. Toast 8 slices of Carrot Wheat Bread. This may be done in a toaster or in the oven with the burgers for 3-4 minutes. Spread the toasted slices with Pecan Butter. Serve each burger in between 2 slices of toasted and buttered Carrot Wheat Bread, accompanied by Celery and Chicory Salad.

Note: A medium-size cleaned rabbit will weigh 1.1-1.25 kg/2½-3 lb. The yield of trimmed meat from such a rabbit will be 300-400 g/10-14 oz which means you will need at least 2 rabbits to complete this recipe. Use the leftover rabbit for a stew or as part of a mixed grill.

Carrot Wheat Bread

Makes 2 loaves (thirty-two 1 cm/½ in slices)

175 ml/6 fl oz milk
40 g/1½ oz unsalted butter, melted, plus
   20 g/¾ oz unsalted butter, softened
2 tablespoons sugar
2 teaspoons salt
5 teaspoons dried yeast
225 ml/8 fl oz warm water
225 g/8 oz carrots, finely grated
75 g/3 oz pecans, toasted and chopped
1 egg, size 3, lightly beaten
225 g/8 oz plain wholemeal flour
550 g/18 oz plain flour

Heat the milk in a small saucepan over a medium-high heat. Bring to the simmer, then remove from heat and add 3 tablespoons melted butter, sugar and salt. Stir to dissolve the sugar. Transfer to a small bowl and allow to cool to room temperature.

In a large stainless steel bowl, dissolve the yeast in the warm water. Allow to stand and foam for 6-7 minutes. Add the milk mixture to the yeast, then stir in the carrots, pecans and egg. Add the wholemeal flour and 125 g/4 oz of the plain flour. Stir until smooth. Add an additional 350 g/12 oz plain flour and combine by hand until the mixture becomes a soft dough.

Knead the dough for 6-8 minutes until smooth and elastic, on a clean, lightly floured work surface, using the remaining plain flour as necessary. Coat the inside of a stainless steel bowl with half the remaining softened but-ter. Place the dough into the bowl and wipe the bowl with the dough. Cover the bowl with cling film and place it in a warm location. Allow the dough to rise for about 1 hour or until it has doubled in size.

On a clean work surface that has been dusted with plain flour, knock back the dough to its original size and divide into 2 equal portions. Form each portion into a loaf, and place each loaf into a 22.5 × 12.5 × 7.5 cm/9 × 5 × 3 in loaf tin that has been coated with 1 teaspoon softened butter. Cover each tin with cling film. Allow the dough to rise in a warm location for 45 minutes until it reaches the top of the loaf tins.

Preheat the oven to 190°C/375°F/Gas 5.

Bake the bread on the middle rack of the oven for 30-35 minutes until golden brown. Cool the loaves in the loaf tins for 15 minutes before removing. When removed, allow to cool to room temperature on wire racks before slicing.

To test if the bread is baked, lightly tap the bottom of the loaf; a hollow sound indicates that the bread is done.

One loaf of this bread will provide both the breadcrumbs for the ground rabbit mixture and the sliced bread on which to serve the burgers. However, Robert believes in taking advantage of a good thing, so his recipe yields 2 loaves. You can freeze the extra loaf or serve it warm on a Sunday morning with Pecan Butter or orange marmalade.

Pecan Butter

Makes 225 g/8 oz

1 teaspoon salt
125 g/4 oz carrots, shredded
25 g/1 oz pecans, toasted and chopped
125 g/4 oz unsalted butter, softened

Bring 750 ml/1¼ pints water and the salt to the boil in a large saucepan over a high heat. Cook the carrots in the boiling water for about 1 minute until tender. Drain the carrots, then transfer to a plate and place, uncovered, in the refrigerator to cool.

In a stainless steel bowl, combine the cooled carrots with the pecans and butter. Stir together until well blended. The butter can be stored covered in the refrigerator for up to 2 weeks.

Celery and Chicory Salad

Serves 4

3 tablespoons sherry vinegar
½ teaspoon celery seeds
½ teaspoon chopped fresh thyme
½ teaspoon salt
¼ teaspoon ground white pepper
125 ml/4 fl oz groundnut oil
2 heads chicory, cored and thinly sliced diagonally
3 sticks celery, thinly sliced diagonally
1 small red onion, thinly sliced

In a stainless steel bowl, whisk together the sherry vinegar, celery seeds, thyme, salt and pepper. Continue to whisk the mixture while pouring in a slow, steady stream of the oil. Add the chicory, celery and red onion. Toss with the dressing to coat lightly, then serve immediately.

> *Chicory oxidizes and discolours quickly. For this reason, the salad should be prepared just prior to cooking the burgers. If you need a bit more time, prepare the salad as directed, but cut and add the chicory to the salad at the last moment. The prepared salad without the chicory will keep covered in the refrigerator for several hours before serving.*

Peacock Alley Tuna Burger
with Sesame Brioche and Sesame Ginger Dressing

Makes 4 burgers

John Doherty
Executive Chef
The Waldorf-Astoria
New York, New York

AS THE YOUNGEST AND ONLY AMERICAN-BORN EXECUTIVE CHEF TO OVERSEE THE KITCHENS OF THE WALDORF-ASTORIA, JOHN DOHERTY IS ACCUSTOMED TO TURNING HEADS. A MODEL OF PROFESSIONALISM AND BONHOMIE, JOHN HAS ALSO BEEN A MODEL OF OTHER SORTS, FEATURED IN *M* MAGAZINE ATTIRED BOTH IN TRADITIONAL CHEF'S GARB AND IN A BUSINESS SUIT IN A PICTORIAL OF CURRENT MEN'S FASHIONS. MOST OF THE TIME, HOWEVER, JOHN CAN BE FOUND SUPERVISING THE WALDORF KITCHENS, WHICH PRODUCE THOUSANDS OF MEALS A DAY FOR SOME OF THE MOST PROMINENT PEOPLE IN THE WORLD.

A garnish of delicate lettuce leaves is particularly compatible with this burger.

These tuna burgers also make wonderful hors d'oeuvres. Serve pan-seared, tiny 15 g/½ oz tuna burgers with a black-olive paste (check your favourite tapenade recipe) on grilled Focaccia (see page 82). Garnish with rocket.

625 g/1¼ lb fresh tuna fillet, cut into 2.5 cm/1 in pieces (or 625 g/1¼ lb minced tuna fillet)
5 tablespoons chopped fresh chives
3 tablespoons finely chopped shallots
1 tablespoon extra-virgin olive oil
1 tablespoon soy sauce
1 tablespoon dry red wine
1 teaspoon grated fresh horseradish
3 dashes Worcestershire sauce
Salt and pepper

If using tuna pieces, mince through a meat mincer fitted with a coarse mincing plate into a large stainless steel bowl.

Gently but thoroughly combine the minced tuna with the chives, shallots, olive oil, soy sauce, red wine, horseradish, Worcestershire sauce and salt and pepper.

Gently form the seasoned minced tuna into four 175 g/6 oz burgers, each 2.5 cm/1 in thick. Cover the burgers with cling film and refrigerate until needed.

Heat a well-seasoned flat griddle or a large non-stick frying pan over a medium–high heat. When hot, cook the burgers for 1½–2 minutes on each side for rare, 2½–3 minutes on each side for medium-rare and about 4 minutes on each side for medium. Toast 8 slices of Sesame Brioche on the griddle or in a non-stick frying pan about 1 minute until golden brown.

Serve the tuna burgers on the toasted Sesame Brioche with a ramekin of Sesame Ginger Dressing on the side.

Sesame Brioche

Makes I loaf (sixteen I cm/¹/₂ in slices)

450 g/1 lb plain flour
2 teaspoons salt
2 tablespoons sesame seeds, toasted, plus
** 1 teaspoon**
2 tablespoons sugar
125 ml/4 fl oz warm water
2 tablespoons dried yeast
4 eggs, size 3
175 g/6 oz unsalted butter, softened, plus
** 1 teaspoon**
1 tablespoon cold water

Sift 350 g/12 oz flour with the salt. Add 2 tablespoons sesame seeds and set aside.

In the bowl of an electric mixer, dissolve the sugar in the warm water. Add the yeast and stir gently to dissolve. Allow the mixture to stand and foam for 2-3 minutes.

Place the mixing bowl on an electric mixer fitted with a dough hook. On top of the yeast mixture, add the sifted flour mixture and 3 eggs. Combine on a low speed for 1 minute. Scrape down the sides of the bowl, then continue to mix on a low speed about 2 minutes until dough forms a ball. Adjust the mixer speed to medium and begin to add 175 g/6 oz butter, 15 g/¹/₂ oz at a time, being certain each amount is thoroughly incorporated before adding the next (for more efficient incorporation of the butter, periodically stop the mixer and pull the dough off the hook). Continue to add the butter until all has been incorporated into the dough.

Remove the bowl from the mixer and also remove the dough hook from the dough. Cover the mixing bowl with a towel and place in a warm location. Allow the dough to rise for 1 hour or until it has doubled in volume. Knock back the dough to its original size, transfer to a pie tin lined with cling film, cover the dough with cling film and place in the freezer for 15 minutes.

Preheat the oven to 160°C/325°F/Gas 3.

Flour a clean work surface with some of the remaining sifted flour. Place the dough on the work surface and divide it into 3 equal pieces. Using your hands, roll each piece into a long rope-like strand about 35-37.5 cm/14-15 in long and 4 cm/1¹/₂ in thick. Plait the 3 pieces of dough together. Coat a loaf tin with the remaining teaspoon of butter. Put the plaited dough into the loaf tin and place in a warm location. Allow the dough to rise about 30 minutes until it has doubled in size. Whisk the remaining egg with 1 tablespoon cold water, then gently and lightly brush the top of the dough with this egg wash. Sprinkle the remaining teaspoon sesame seeds over the top of the dough.

Bake the brioche loaf in the centre of the oven for 30 minutes. Allow the baked loaf to cool in the tin for 15 minutes before removing from tin. Remove the brioche from the loaf tin and allow to cool to room temperature before slicing.

To test if the brioche is baked, gently remove the loaf from the baking tin. Lightly tap the base of the loaf; a hollow sound will indicate that the bread is done.

> *An electric mixer fitted with a dough hook is an essential piece of equipment for the successful preparation of high-quality brioche, a yeast-raised bread enriched with eggs. If such a mixer is not in residence in your equipment cupboard, consider an alternative bread, such as traditional challah.*

Sesame Ginger Dressing

Makes about 225 ml/8 fl oz

50 ml/2 fl oz water
1 teaspoon sugar
1 teaspoon finely chopped fresh ginger
175 g/6 oz mayonnaise
1 tablespoon sesame oil (see Note)
Salt and pepper

Bring the water and sugar to the boil in a large saucepan. Add the ginger and allow to cook for about 1 minute until the ginger is tender. Remove the mixture from the heat and cool in an ice-water bath.

In a stainless steel bowl, whisk together the mayonnaise and cold ginger-water mixture. Slowly whisk the sesame oil into the ginger-mayonnaise mixture. Adjust the seasoning with salt and pepper, and combine thoroughly. Cover with cling film and refrigerate for at least 6 hours before using.

Note: Look for sesame oil in Asian grocery shops or your local supermarket. Purchase oil that is packaged in glass bottles or cans rather than plastic bottles, as the oil has a tendency to turn rancid more quickly in plastic packaging.

Sesame Ginger Dressing will add a piquant and delicious touch to your favourite salad, as well as to John Doherty's delicious tuna burger.

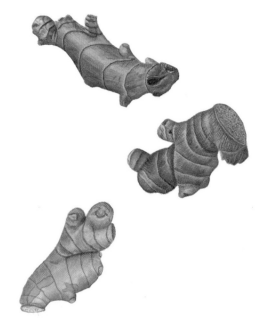

Southern Fried Chicken Burger
with Honey Mustard Mayonnaise and
Toasted Peanut and Sweetcorn Salad

Makes 4 burgers

Mark Erickson
Executive Chef
Cherokee Town and Country Club
Atlanta, Georgia

AFTER WORKING AS SOUS CHEF AT THE GREENBRIER RESORT IN WHITE SULPHUR SPRINGS, WEST VIRGINIA, IN THE EARLY 1980S, MARK RETURNED TO THE CULINARY INSTITUTE OF AMERICA TO TEACH. A CERTIFIED MASTER CHEF, HE WAS ALSO THE OPENING CHEF FOR THE INSTITUTE'S NUTRITIONAL RESTAURANT, THE SAINT ANDREW'S CAFE. IN 1990, MARK BECAME THE EXECUTIVE CHEF OF THE CHEROKEE TOWN AND COUNTRY CLUB IN ATLANTA, WHERE HE IS PUTTING A NEW TWIST TO REGIONAL CUISINE. WITH THIS RECIPE, HE OFFERS GUESTS OF THE VENERABLE CLUB SOME REAL "SOUTHERN COMFORT".

If you are not in the mood for a ground chicken burger, then Mark suggests using a whole 125 g/4 oz boneless and skinless chicken breast. You may either pan-sear or grill the breast. But, of course, frying it as suggested for the chicken burger will also result in good eating.

625 g/1¼ lb boneless and skinless chicken breast meat, trimmed of fat and cut into 2.5 cm/1 in pieces (or 625 g/1¼ lb minced chicken breast meat)
1 egg white, size 3
3 tablespoons buttermilk
1 small clove garlic, finely chopped
1 teaspoon salt

1 teaspoon freshly ground black pepper
175 g/6 oz dry breadcrumbs
225 g/8 oz groundnut oil
4 Best Burger Buns (see page 109), cut in half, or 8 slices cornbread
8 iceberg lettuce leaves, washed and dried
4 slices ripe tomatoes

If using chicken pieces, mince through a meat mincer fitted with a coarse mincing plate into a large stainless steel bowl.

In a separate bowl, whisk together the egg white, buttermilk, garlic, salt and pepper. Add this mixture and 50 g/2 oz breadcrumbs to the minced chicken meat. Combine the ingredients gently but thoroughly.

Gently form the chicken mixture into four 150 g/5 oz burgers, each 2.5 cm/1 in thick. Cover the burgers with cling film and refrigerate until needed.

Preheat the oven to 150°C/300°F/Gas 2.

Heat the oil in a large non-stick frying pan over a medium-high heat. Lightly coat the chicken burgers with the remaining breadcrumbs. When the oil is hot, cook 2 of the burgers at a time for 1 minute on each side. Place the chicken burgers on a baking sheet in the oven for 12-14 minutes.

Toast the buns, cut sides down, in a non-stick frying pan over a medium-high heat until golden brown.

Spread each top and bottom bun half with Honey Mustard Mayonnaise. Place a chicken burger on the bottom half of each bun. Top each burger with 2 of the lettuce leaves and a slice of the tomato. Top with the other half of the bun and serve with Toasted Peanut and Sweetcorn Salad.

Honey Mustard Mayonnaise

Makes about 300 g/10 oz

175 g/6 oz mayonnaise
6 tablespoons spicy brown mustard
3 tablespoons honey
Salt and pepper

In a stainless steel bowl, whisk together the mayonnaise, mustard, and honey. Adjust the seasoning with salt and pepper, then combine thoroughly. Cover with cling film and refrigerate until needed.

> *This easily prepared condiment is also good with other foods. Try it as an accompaniment to a full-flavoured fish such as tuna or as a spread on your favourite sandwich (it is quite good with smoked turkey).*

Toasted Peanut and Sweetcorn Salad

Makes about 450 g/1 lb

175 g/6 oz unsalted shelled peanuts
3 medium ears fresh yellow corn, husks and silks removed
75 ml/3 fl oz groundnut oil
2 tablespoons cider vinegar
1 small red onion, finely chopped
1 tablespoon chopped fresh parsley
Salt and pepper

Preheat the oven to 150°C/300°F/Gas 2.

Toast the peanuts on a baking sheet in the oven for 20-25 minutes until golden brown. Keep at room temperature until needed.

Blanch the corn for 2-3 minutes in a large pan of boiling salted water. Drain and cool under cold running water. When the corn is cool enough to handle, cut away the kernels.

In a stainless steel bowl, whisk together the groundnut oil and cider vinegar. Add the toasted peanuts, corn kernels, red onion and parsley. Adjust the seasoning with salt and pepper, then combine thoroughly. Cover with cling film and refrigerate for several hours before using.

> *This salad would also be terrific as a side dish with pork chops. Conjure up visions of pork chops basted with groundnut oil, slowly cooking over the embers of a wood fire, and you might just find yourself in Mark Erickson's neighbourhood.*

Mansion Roadhouse Burger
with Dean's Favourite French Fries

Makes 4 burgers

Dean Fearing
Chef
The Mansion on Turtle Creek
Dallas, Texas

DEAN FEARING CONSISTENTLY DAZZLES THE PALATES OF DINERS AT THE INTERNATIONALLY KNOWN MANSION ON TURTLE CREEK IN DALLAS, WHERE HE HAS BEEN EXECUTIVE CHEF SINCE 1987. DEAN'S TRADEMARK IS NEW SOUTH-WEST CUISINE, WHICH HE PIONEERED IN DALLAS IN THE EARLY 1980S. DEAN SHARES HIS IMAGINATIVE CUISINE IN TWO COOKBOOKS: *THE MANSION ON TURTLE CREEK COOKBOOK* AND *DEAN FEARING'S SOUTHWEST CUISINE.*

THE MANSION ROADHOUSE BURGER RECIPE IS DEAN'S SALUTE TO THE ROADHOUSE CAFÉS AND TRUCK STOPS IN TEXAS WHERE THE DOUBLE CHEESEBURGER BECAME FAMOUS.

> *Dean admits that his Mansion Roadhouse Burger is a substantial handful, even for Texans. He suggests that you not wear your favourite silk blouse or shirt for this gustatory adventure.*

900 g/2 lb lean minced beef
Salt and pepper
25 g/1 oz unsalted butter, melted
8 slices processed Cheddar cheese
4 Best Burger Buns (see page 109), cut in half
2 tablespoons mayonnaise
2 tablespoons yellow mustard
8 iceberg lettuce leaves, washed and dried
4 slices ripe tomatoes
4 slices onions
16 gherkin slices

Gently form the minced beef into eight 125 g/4 oz burgers, each 1 cm/½ in thick. Season each with salt and pepper. Cover the burgers with cling film and refrigerate until needed.

Preheat the oven to 190°C/375°F/Gas 5.

Brush each bun half with the butter. Place the buns, buttered sides up, on a baking tray and bake until golden brown. Reduce the oven heat to keep the buns warm until needed.

Heat a well-seasoned flat griddle or a large non-stick frying pan over a medium-high heat. When hot, cook the burgers for 3 minutes on one side. Turn the burgers over and place 1 slice of the processed cheese on each burger. (This cooking time will yield a medium-rare burger. For rare, cook 2 minutes before turning; for medium, cook about 3½ minutes before turning.) While the cheese is melting, remove the buns from the oven and spread each top bun with mayonnaise and each bottom bun with mustard. When the cheese has melted, place 2 of the burgers, one on top of the other, on the bottom half of each bun. Top each stack of burgers with 2 of the lettuce leaves, 1 slice each of tomato and onion and 4 of the gherkin slices. Top with the other half of the bun and serve with Dean's Favourite French Fries and a bottle of ketchup.

Dean's Favourite French Fries

Serves 4

**6 large potatoes, such as Maris Piper, washed
  and scrubbed clean**
Vegetable oil for deep-frying
225 g/8 oz plain flour
2 teaspoons cayenne
2 teaspoons chopped fresh thyme
¹/₂ teaspoon chopped fresh sage
¹/₂ teaspoon salt
¹/₄ teaspoon ground white pepper
1 cup milk
Salt and pepper

Preheat the oven to 220°C/425°F/Gas 7.

Use a skewer to pierce the skin of each potato several times (this will prevent the skin from cracking during baking). Place the potatoes on the centre rack of the oven and bake them for about 1¹/₄ hours until soft to the touch when gently squeezed. Remove the potatoes from the oven and allow them to cool to room temperature.

When the potatoes are cool, use a sharp knife to cut each one into sixths lengthways. Cover with cling film and refrigerate until needed. (The cooled and cut potatoes may be kept refrigerated for a couple of days before using.)

Heat the vegetable oil in a deep-fat fryer (or high-sided, heavy-based saucepan) fitted with a deep-fat frying basket over a high heat to a temperature of 185°C/360°F.

Thoroughly combine the flour with cayenne pepper, thyme, sage, ¹/₂ teaspoon salt and ground white pepper.

Dip the potatoes into the milk and then into the seasoned flour mixture; coat evenly, lightly and thoroughly. Fry the potatoes in the hot oil, one-quarter at a time, for 1-1¹/₂ minutes until potatoes are golden brown and crisp. Drain potatoes on kitchen paper. Lightly season with salt and pepper, and serve immediately.

The fried potatoes may be kept warm in a 120°C/250°F/Gas ¹/₂ oven for 15-20 minutes before serving.

This recipe is proportioned for spud lovers. If your appetite is not Texan in nature, use 4 spuds rather than 6.

New England Maple Barbecued Pork Burger
with Anadama Rolls and Celeriac Chips

Makes 8 burgers

Phyllis Flaherty-Bologna
*Executive Chef for National Accounts
Development
General Foods Foodservice
White Plains, New York*

SEVERAL YEARS AFTER GRADUATION, PHYLLIS FLAHERTY-BOLOGNA RETURNED TO THE CULINARY INSTITUTE OF AMERICA AND SERVED ON ITS FACULTY FOR FIVE YEARS. IN 1987, SHE TOOK THE EXTREMELY CHALLENGING POSITION AS EXECUTIVE CHEF FOR GENERAL FOODS USA.

PLAYING ON THE OLD ADAGE THAT "THE PROOF IS IN THE PUDDING", PHYLLIS BELIEVES THAT THE "PROOF OF THE BURGER IS IN THE BUN". HER ANADAMA ROLLS—HOME BASE FOR HER NEW ENGLAND MAPLE BARBECUED PORK BURGER—CONFIRM HER THEORY.

1.1 kg/2½ lb trimmed fresh pork fillet, cut into 2.5 cm/ 1 in pieces (or 1.1 kg/2½ lb minced trimmed pork fillet)
2 teaspoons dry mustard
½ teaspoon dried red chilli flakes
Salt and white pepper

125 ml/4 fl oz barbecue sauce (use your favourite sauce or see page 46 for Quick Barbecue Sauce)
150 g/5 oz maple syrup
1 tablespoon cider vinegar
1 tablespoon brown sugar
1 teaspoon lemon juice
¼ teaspoon grated lemon rind
2 tablespoons unsalted butter, melted

If using pork pieces, mince through a meat mincer fitted with a coarse mincing plate into a large stainless steel bowl.

Gently but thoroughly combine the minced pork with the dry mustard, red chilli flakes and salt and pepper to taste.

Gently form the seasoned pork into eight 150 g/5 oz burgers, each 2.5 cm/ 1 in thick. Cover the burgers with cling film and refrigerate until needed.

Prepare the maple glaze. Heat the barbecue sauce, maple syrup, cider vinegar, brown sugar, lemon juice and lemon rind in a saucepan over a medium-high heat. Bring the mixture to the boil, then adjust the heat and allow to simmer for 10 minutes until slightly thickened.

Preheat the oven to 160°C/325°F/Gas 3.

Heat a well-seasoned flat griddle or a large non-stick frying pan over a medium-high heat. When hot, sear the burgers until well browned on each side. Remove the burgers to a large ovenproof pan and baste with one-half of the maple glaze. Place the pan in the oven and allow to cook for 20-22 minutes.

Cut 8 Anadama Rolls in half. Brush each roll half with melted butter. Toast the rolls, buttered sides down, on the griddle or in a non-stick frying pan over a medium-high heat until golden brown.

Remove the burgers from the oven. Place a pork burger on the bottom half of each roll. Baste the burgers with the remaining maple glaze. Top with the other half of the roll and serve with Celeriac Chips.

Anadama Rolls

Makes 12 rolls

750 g/1½ lb plain flour
125 g/4 oz yellow cornmeal, plus 4 tablespoons
1 tablespoon dried yeast
2½ teaspoons salt
50 g/2 oz unsalted butter
450 ml/¾ pint water, plus 1 tablespoon
125 g/4 oz molasses
1 egg yolk, size 3

Combine all but 50 g/2 oz of the flour, 125 g/4 oz corn-meal, yeast and salt in the bowl of an electric mixer fitted with a paddle.

With the mixer on a low speed, add the butter, 15 g/½ oz at a time and combine the ingredients until the mixture resembles fine crumbs. Remove the paddle from the mixer and replace with a dough hook. (If a table-model electric mixer is not available, follow the directions using a hand-held mixer or kneading by hand. The mixing times will increase depending upon which alternative method is used.)

Combine 450 ml/¾ pint hot water (about 55°C/130°F) and the molasses in a bowl. Stir with a whisk to dissolve the molasses. Add the molasses mixture to the dry ingredients. Mix on a low speed for 5 minutes, stopping the mixer at 1 minute intervals and thoroughly scraping down the sides of the bowl. Mix for an additional 2-3 minutes on a medium-low speed until the dough is smooth and no longer sticky.

Remove the bowl from the mixer and cover with a towel or cling film. Allow the dough to rise in a warm location for 1 hour until it has doubled in volume.

Place the dough on a clean, lightly floured work surface, using the remaining flour as necessary. Use a sharp knife to cut the dough into 12 equal portions. Shape each portion into a round ball. Divide the dough balls on to 2 baking trays lined with baking parchment. Dust each dough ball with 1 teaspoon cornmeal. Allow to rise in a warm location for 25-30 minutes until doubled in size.

Preheat the oven to 180°C/350°F/Gas 4.

Use a razor blade or a very sharp paring knife to cut a 0.5 cm/¼ in deep slit into the top of each roll. Whisk together the egg yolk and 1 tablespoon cold water, then gently and lightly brush the top of each dough ball with this egg wash.

Bake the rolls for 25-30 minutes, rotating the trays from top to bottom and front to back about halfway through the baking time.

Allow the rolls to cool thoroughly before cutting in half.

The rolls will keep fresh for 2 or 3 days stored in a sealed polythene bag at room temperature.

According to the oft-repeated tale of the origin of anadama bread, it was a New England fisherman's endearment—or perhaps his lack thereof—for his wife and her fondness for baking molasses bread that led to the epitaph "Anna was a lovely bride, but Anna, damn 'er, up and died". Apocryphal as this anecdote may be, this unique bread derives much character from molasses and cornmeal, and it is particularly good with Phyllis Flaherty-Bologna's burger.

Celeriac Chips

Serves 8

900 g/2 lb celeriac, trimmed (see Note)
1 whole lemon, cut in half
Vegetable oil for deep-frying
Salt and pepper

Peel the outer skin from each celeriac. Immediately rub each root with the cut end of a lemon half to prevent discolouration.

Using a mandoline or a very sharp stainless steel knife, slice the celeriac very thin, immediately placing the slices in ice water to prevent discoloration.

Heat the vegetable oil in a deep-fat fryer (or high-sided, heavy-based saucepan) fitted with a deep-frying basket over a high heat to a temperature of 200°C/400°F. (To produce light, crispy and greaseless chips, it is necessary to fry them at this temperature. The oil will probably need to be discarded after all the chips for this recipe have been fried, as the high heat will shorten its lifespan.)

Drain the celeriac slices in a colander and pat dry between kitchen towels.

Fry one-eighth of the celeriac slices for 1-1½ minutes until golden brown and crisp. Transfer the fried slices to kitchen towels to drain. Repeat the frying procedure with the remaining batches of sliced celeriac, waiting about 1 minute before frying each new batch to allow the oil to return to 200°C/400°F. Season with salt and pepper. Serve immediately.

The chips will keep warm and crisp in an oven set on warm for up to 2 hours. Do not salt the chips after they have been fried if you plan on keeping them in the oven; salt just before serving.

Note: Celeriac is also known variously as celery root and knob celery. Purchase roots that are firm and have a clean and slightly celery-scented smell; avoid those that have a damp and musty aroma.

A typical medium-size celery root (trimmed of leaves and stalks) will weigh 225-300 g/8-10 oz and be 9-10 cm/3½-4 in in diameter.

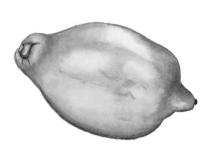
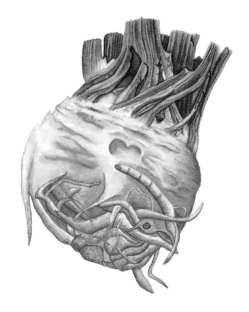

Fillet of Beef Burger
with Yellow Corn Salsa

Makes 8 burgers

Larry Forgione
Chef/Owner
An American Place
New York, New York

HAILED AS ONE OF THE PIONEERS OF THE NEW AMERICAN CUISINE, LARRY FORGIONE HAS ESTABLISHED THE CRITERIA FOR INNOVATIVE YOUNG CULINARIANS IN AMERICA. HIS UNSTINTING USE OF AMERICAN INGREDIENTS HAS ENCOURAGED SMALL FARM PRODUCERS TO GROW AND CULTIVATE A CONSTANTLY EXPANDING LIST OF UNIQUE AND DELECTABLE FOODS.

IN 1983, LARRY OPENED AN AMERICAN PLACE, WHICH FEATURES ONLY AMERICAN-GROWN AND -PRODUCED PRODUCTS. HE IS ALSO A PARTNER IN THE BEEKMAN 1766 TAVERN AT THE BEEKMAN ARMS IN RHINEBECK, NEW YORK, AND A CO-FOUNDER OF AMERICAN SPOON FOODS, A SPECIALITY FOOD COMPANY.

LARRY'S FILLET OF BEEF BURGER IS A SOPHISTICATED VERSION OF AN AMERICAN FAVOURITE.

750 g/1½ lb lean beef chuck, cut into 2.5 cm/1 in pieces (or 750 g/1½ lb minced lean beef)

1 ripe avocado, 175-200 g/6-7 oz

4 tablespoons barbecue sauce or other favourite sauce (see page 46 for Quick Barbecue Sauce)

2 tablespoons chopped fresh flat-leaf parsley

1 tablespoon chopped fresh coriander

1 tablespoon olive oil

1 teaspoon salt

1 teaspoon freshly ground black pepper

8 Best Burger Buns (see page 109), cut in half

If using beef pieces, mince through a meat mincer fitted with a coarse mincing plate into a large stainless steel bowl.

Cut, seed and peel the avocado. Finely chop the avocado flesh.

Gently but thoroughly combine the minced beef with the avocado pieces, barbecue sauce, parsley, coriander, olive oil, salt and pepper.

Gently form the meat-avocado mixture into eight 125 g/4 oz burgers, each 3 cm/1¼ in thick. Cover the burgers with cling film and refrigerate until needed.

Heat a well-seasoned flat griddle or a large non-stick frying pan over a medium-high heat. When hot, cook the burgers as desired: 3-4 minutes on each side for rare, 5-6 minutes on each side for medium and 8-9 minutes on each side for well done.

Toast the buns, cut sides down, on the griddle or in a non-stick frying pan until golden brown. Serve the burgers on the toasted buns accompanied by Yellow Corn Salsa.

Yellow Corn Salsa

Serves 8

4 large ears yellow sweetcorn, husks and silks removed
2 small, hot red or green chillies, roasted, skinned, seeded and finely chopped
2 whole fresh limes
150 g/5 oz finely diced green pepper
150 g/5 oz finely diced red pepper
2 tablespoons chopped fresh coriander
Salt and freshly ground black pepper

Cook the corn for 4 minutes in boiling salted water. Drain, then cool under cold running water. When the corn is cool enough to handle, cut away the kernels. Cover with cling film and set aside until needed.

In a large stainless steel bowl, combine the corn and chillies. Cut the limes in half and squeeze the juice on to the corn. Add the green pepper, red pepper and coriander. Season with salt and freshly ground black pepper. Keep the salsa at room temperature covered with cling film for up to 2 hours before serving.

The spirited flavours of this salsa seem to be at their peak when it is freshly prepared. It may, however, be made in advance with a minimum loss of flavour. Keep the salsa tightly covered in the refrigerator for 2 or 3 days. Allow it to stand at room temperature for 30-40 minutes before serving (the flavours of this mixture are heightened by being served at room temperature rather than chilled).

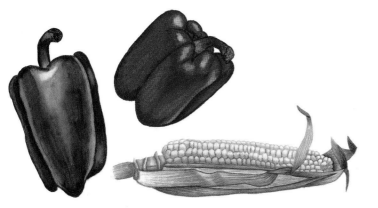

Virgin Island Cod Burger
with Avocado and Tomato Relish and Okra Fungee

Makes 4 burgers

Jacqueline Frazer
Personal Caterer
New York, New York

WITH A DISTINCTIVE STYLE, VARIED MENUS
AND IMAGINATIVE PRESENTATIONS,
JACQUELINE FRAZER IS ONE OF THE MOST
SOUGHT-AFTER CHEFS FOR PRIVATE DINING
AND BUSINESS ENTERTAINING IN THE NEW
YORK METROPOLITAN AREA.

WITH A CLIENT LIST THAT REFLECTS
NEW YORK'S MOVERS AND SHAKERS,
JACQUELINE HAS SPENT HER YEARS SINCE
GRADUATION PLEASING THE PALATES OF
SUCH WELL-KNOWN PEOPLE AS LEONA
AND HARRY HELMSLEY (SHE WAS THEIR
PRIVATE CHEF IN 1986 AND 1987) AND, MORE
RECENTLY, PUBLISHING MOGUL WILLIAM
RANDOLPH HEARST, JR.

JACQUELINE'S VIRGIN ISLAND COD
BURGER IS A CONTEMPORARY
INTERPRETATION OF A TRADITIONAL
CARIBBEAN RECIPE FOR SALT COD CAKES
THAT MAKES THE MOST OF FRESH COD.

This cod burger tantalizes the taste buds. Although the flavours are not bashful, they leave a subtle and pleasant taste lingering on the palate. Such interesting food calls for an equally appealing beverage. A cold ginger beer is great, but an even better suggestion is what Jacqueline calls an Island Manhattan—50 ml/2 fl oz medium-dark rum and 25 ml/1 fl oz of sweet vermouth stirred with a few ice cubes.

---

2 teaspoons salt
1 small potato
450 g/1 lb fresh cod fillet, cut into 0.5 cm/¼ in dice
65 g/2½ oz onion, finely chopped
1 egg, size 3, lightly beaten
2 spring onions, trimmed and thinly sliced
1 tablespoon chopped fresh parsley
½ teaspoon chopped fresh thyme
½ teaspoon dried red pepper flakes
¼ teaspoon white pepper
125 ml/4 fl oz olive oil
50 g/2 oz yellow cornmeal
8 small flour tortillas (see page 130; follow the recipe as directed, but omit the sage)

Bring a large saucepan of water with 1 teaspoon salt to the boil. Meanwhile, peel the potato, then rinse with cold water. When the water boils, add the potato, adjust the heat and allow the potato to simmer for 35 minutes until cooked through. Remove the potato from the water, cut in half lengthways and cool, uncovered, in the refrigerator. When thoroughly cooled, grate the potato using a hand grater. Refrigerate until ready to assemble the burger.

In a large stainless steel bowl, gently but thoroughly combine the cod, grated potatoes, onions, egg, spring onions, parsley, remaining 1 teaspoon salt, thyme, red chilli flakes and pepper.

Gently form the cod mixture into four 175 g/6 oz burgers, each 2.5 cm/ 1 in thick. Cover the burgers with cling film and refrigerate until needed.

Preheat the oven to 200°C/400°F/Gas 6.

Heat the olive oil in a large non-stick frying pan over a medium-high heat. While the oil is heating, lightly coat the cod burgers with the cornmeal. When the oil is hot, place the cod burgers in the pan. Pan-fry the burgers for about 2 minutes on each side until golden brown. Transfer to a baking tray and place in the oven for 10 minutes until cooked through.

Cook the tortillas, 4 at a time, in a large non-stick frying pan over a medium-high heat for 1 minute on each side until lightly browned.

Place each cod burger on a tortilla. Top each burger with 1-2 tablespoons Avocado and Tomato Relish and another tortilla. Serve accompanied by the Okra Fungee.

Avocado and Tomato Relish

Makes about 300 g/10 oz

1 avocado
1 small hot, red or green chilli, roasted,
  skinned, seeded and finely chopped
1 small ripe red tomato, peeled, seeded
  and chopped
40 g/1½ oz red onion, very finely chopped
1 spring onion, thinly sliced
2 tablespoons extra-virgin olive oil
½ tablespoon chopped fresh parsley
1 teaspoon chopped fresh coriander
½ teaspoon finely chopped garlic
  Juice of ½ lime
  Salt and pepper

Cut, seed and peel the avocado. Cut the avocado halves into 0.5 cm/¼ in pieces.

In a large stainless steel bowl, combine the avocado, chilli, tomato, red onions, spring onions, olive oil, parsley, coriander and garlic. Add the lime juice and season with salt and pepper. Gently but thoroughly combine the mixture. Serve immediately. The Avocado and Tomato Relish may be kept covered in the refrigerator for several hours before serving.

> *This relish is a perfect condiment for Jacqueline's cod burger. No need to limit its use to the burger, however. It is wonderful with grilled fish and is an ideal accompaniment to a salad of grilled chicken breast with assorted greens and grilled red onions (brush the onions with olive oil and season liberally with salt and pepper before grilling).*

Okra Fungee

Serves 4

125 g/4 oz yellow cornmeal
1½ teaspoons salt
½ teaspoon white pepper
  Pinch cayenne pepper
125 g/4 oz fresh okra, stalks removed and sliced
50 g/2 oz unsalted butter

In a small stainless steel bowl, combine the cornmeal with 225 ml/8 fl oz cold water.

Heat 350 ml/12 fl oz water with the salt, white pepper and cayenne pepper in a saucepan over a high heat. Bring to the boil, then add the okra and cook for 2 minutes. Add the cornmeal-water mixture. Bring the mixture to the boil, then reduce the heat to medium-low. Continue cooking, stirring constantly, for 3-4 minutes until the mixture releases itself from the sides of the pan. Stir in the butter and serve immediately.

> *Okra Fungee, which Jacqueline calls "Caribbean mashed potatoes", is an extraordinarily delicious recipe that, like polenta, may be cooled, sliced and pan-fried. For pan-fried Okra Fungee, cool the mixture on a baking sheet, spreading it out while still hot to a thickness of 1-2 cm/½-¾ in. When cool, cut it into 8 pieces, each 5 × 6 cm/2 × 2½ in. Lightly brush a large non-stick frying pan with olive oil. Heat the pan over a medium-high heat. When the pan is hot, fry the Okra Fungee pieces for 2½-3 minutes on each side. Serve hot and crisp.*

Steak Chilli Burger
with Smoky Coleslaw and Black Bean Chilli

Makes 6 burgers

Kevin Garvin
Executive Chef
The Adolphus Hotel
Dallas, Texas

KEVIN GARVIN, WHOSE TECHNIQUES WERE CALLED "SMART AND ENERGETIC" AND WHOSE MAIN COURSES WERE DESCRIBED AS "DEVASTATINGLY DELICIOUS" IN A RECENT REVIEW, IS CUTTING A SWATH THROUGH THE FOOD WORLD OF DALLAS AND THE UNITED STATES.

WHEN THE *DALLAS MORNING NEWS* LISTED KEVIN AMONG THE YOUNG CHEFS TO WATCH IN THE 1990S, IT WAS HEDGING ITS BET. ALTHOUGH HE IS A YOUNG MAN, HIS YOUTH BELIES THE YEARS OF EXPERIENCE ALREADY UNDER HIS BELT.

BEFORE JOINING THE ADOLPHUS IN 1988, CHEF GARVIN HELD EXECUTIVE CHEF POSITIONS AT SEVERAL OTHER LUXURY HOTELS THROUGHOUT THE UNITED STATES. NOW ENSCONCED AT THE ADOLPHUS, KEVIN HAS DEVELOPED A CULINARY IDENTITY FOR THE HOTEL'S THREE RESTAURANTS. HE HAS ALSO EMERGED AS ONE OF DALLAS' MOST POPULAR TEACHING CHEFS.

IN MAY 1991, KEVIN WAS CHOSEN BY BUCKINGHAM PALACE TO PREPARE A PRIVATE LUNCHEON FOR HER MAJESTY QUEEN ELIZABETH II AND HIS ROYAL HIGHNESS PRINCE PHILIP, THE DUKE OF EDINBURGH.

BUT BACK HOME, KEVIN'S BURGER IMPARTS THE TRUE FLAVOURS OF THE AMERICAN SOUTH-WEST.

900 g/2 lb tender steak, such as topside, cut into 1 cm/½ in pieces (or 900 g/2 lb minced steak)
½ teaspoon salt
1 teaspoon ground cumin
¼ teaspoon cayenne pepper
3 tablespoons vegetable oil
1 tablespoon finely chopped garlic
1 green pepper, seeded and diced

1 red pepper, seeded and diced
4 tablespoons masa harina (very fine cornmeal)
2 tablespoons plain flour
Salt and pepper
6 Best Burger Buns (see page 109), cut in half

If using steak pieces, mince through a meat mincer fitted with a coarse mincing plate into a large stainless steel bowl. Season the minced steak with the salt, cumin and cayenne pepper. Cover with cling film and refrigerate until needed.

Heat 1 tablespoon vegetable oil in a medium non-stick frying pan over a medium-high heat. When hot, add the garlic and cook for 30 seconds. Add the green pepper and red pepper and continue to cook an additional 3-4 minutes, stirring frequently to avoid browning the garlic, until the peppers are tender. Transfer the mixture to a plate and place, uncovered, in the refrigerator to cool.

Add the cooled pepper-garlic mixture to the seasoned minced meat and gently but thoroughly combine the ingredients.

Gently form the meat-pepper mixture into six 150-175 g/5-6 oz burgers, each 2.5 cm/1 in thick. Cover the burgers with cling film and refrigerate until needed.

Preheat the oven to 190°C/375°F/Gas 5.

Combine the masa harina and flour. Season with salt and pepper and combine thoroughly.

Heat the remaining 2 tablespoons vegetable oil in a large non-stick frying pan over a medium-high heat. While the oil is heating, place the burgers into the masa harina–flour mixture; coat evenly and thoroughly. When the oil is hot, pan-fry the burgers in the vegetable oil, 3 at a time, for about 3 minutes

Kevin Garvin also enjoys serving his Steak Chilli Burgers on multi-grain buns.

on each side until lightly browned. Transfer to a baking tray and place in the oven: 3-4 minutes for rare, 8-9 minutes for medium and 10-12 minutes for well done.

(If you prefer to grill the hamburgers, omit the masa harina–flour coating. Prior to grilling, season the burgers with salt and pepper. Grill the burgers over a medium wood or charcoal fire. Cook as desired: 3-4 minutes on each side for medium-rare, 5-6 minutes on each side for medium and 8-9 minutes on each side for well done.)

While the burgers are cooking, toast the buns in the oven until golden brown.

Place the burgers on the buns, top generously with Black Bean Chilli and serve accompanied by Smoky Coleslaw.

Smoky Coleslaw

Serves 4

    1 cup hickory wood chips, about 150 g/5 oz
    1 tablespoon grated fresh horseradish
    2 tablespoons cider vinegar
125 g/4 oz mayonnaise
    3 spring onions, trimmed and thinly sliced
      diagonally
      Salt and pepper
  ¼ red cabbage, cored
  ¼ white cabbage, cored
    3 carrots, peeled and cut lengthways
    2 green chillies, split, stalks removed and
      seeded

Soak the hickory chips in cold water for at least 15 minutes. Drain well.

In a large stainless steel bowl, whisk together the horseradish, cider vinegar, mayonnaise and spring onions. Adjust the seasoning with salt and pepper and combine

thoroughly. Cover this dressing with cling film and refrigerate until needed.

Prepare a small wood or charcoal fire in the grill. Allow the coals to mellow to a medium-low fire, then spread the coals evenly over the bottom of the grill. Sprinkle the soaked hickory chips on to the coals. While waiting for the chips to begin smoldering, arrange the vegetables on the grill rack. Place the rack with the vegetables on the grill. Cover the grill and smoke the vegetables for 15-20 minutes. (For a more profoundly smoky flavour, smoke the vegetables on the grill for an additional 5-10 minutes.)

Remove the vegetables from the grill and cool to room temperature.

Grate the vegetables in a food processor fitted with a medium grating disc.

Add the grated vegetables to the dressing, season with salt and pepper and combine thoroughly. Serve the coleslaw immediately.

The coleslaw will keep tightly covered in the refrigerator for 1 or 2 days.

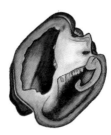

Black Bean Chilli

Makes about 400 g/14 oz

175 g/6 oz dried black beans, washed and
    picked over
1 tablespoon salt
1 tablespoon vegetable oil
2 small dried hot red or green chillies, stalks
    removed, seeded and chopped
140 g/4½ oz tomato purée
2 tablespoons Ancho Paste (see following
    recipe)
2 tablespoons honey
Salt

Soak the black beans overnight in water to cover. Drain
the beans thoroughly before cooking.

Bring a large saucepan of water with 1 tablespoon salt
to the boil over a high heat. When the water boils, add the
beans. Reduce the heat and simmer for about 30 minutes
until the beans are tender. Drain the cooked beans in a
colander. Set aside until needed.

Heat the vegetable oil in a medium non-stick frying
pan over a medium heat. When hot, add the chillies and
cook for 1 minute. Add the tomato purée and Ancho Paste
and cook, stirring constantly, for 3 minutes. Add the
beans and honey. Season with salt. Continue to cook for
10 minutes. Serve immediately, or cool in an ice-water
bath and refrigerate, tightly covered, for up to several
days. When ready to re-heat, add 1-2 tablespoons water
and adjust the seasoning, if necessary. Serve hot.

Ancho Paste

Makes about 175 g/6 oz

1 medium hot green or red chilli, roasted,
    skinned and seeded
5 dried ancho chillies, stalks removed and
    seeded (see Note)
65 g/2½ oz onion, chopped
1 clove garlic, peeled
225 ml/8 fl oz water

Heat all the ingredients in a saucepan over a high heat.
When the mixture comes to a boil, adjust the heat and
allow to simmer about 15 minutes until the ancho chillies
are soft.

Purée the hot chilli mixture in a food processor fitted
with a metal blade until smooth. Strain the purée through
a sieve. Use immediately or cool to room temperature
before refrigerating, tightly covered, in a non-corrosive
container. The paste will keep in the refrigerator for
several weeks.

Note: Although the deep red colour of the ancho
chilli gives a murderous appearance to the paste, this chilli
is relatively mild in flavour. Look for ancho chillies in
speciality food stores, or substitute another mildly hot
dried chilli.

Salmon Burger
with Pernod, Mustard and Dill Mayonnaise; Fennel and Red Onion Salad; and Sweet Potato Fries

Makes 4 burgers

John A. Halligan
Executive Chef
Rihga Royal Hotel
New York, New York

LANDMARK HOTELS HAVE BEEN JOHN HALLIGAN'S CULINARY PATH. AFTER GRADUATING FROM THE INSTITUTE, HE WENT TO WORK IN NEW YORK CITY AT THE REGENCY HOTEL ON PARK AVENUE, THEN THE HELMSLEY PARK LANE HOTEL ON CENTRAL PARK. IN 1988, JOHN OPENED THE EXCLUSIVE ST. JAMES'S CLUB AND HOTEL IN LOS ANGELES WHILE ALSO WORKING AS CONSULTANT TO THE OTHER ST. JAMES'S CLUBS IN PARIS, LONDON AND ANTIGUA.

INSTEAD OF SPECIALIZING IN A SPECIFIC STYLE OF COOKING, JOHN STUDIES A WIDE VARIETY OF PREPARATION TECHNIQUES AND CUISINES. HE FEELS THAT TODAY'S FOOD SHOULD BE HEALTHY, ECLECTIC, IMAGINATIVE, UNRESTRICTED BY ETHNIC BOUNDARIES AND ALWAYS EXPANDING; THIS PHILOSOPHY IS REFLECTED IN THE CUISINE AT THE RIHGA ROYAL HOTEL, ESPECIALLY THAT OF ITS HALCYON RESTAURANT.

JOHN'S SALMON BURGER ADDS QUITE A BIT OF SOPHISTICATION TO THIS ALL-AMERICAN FARE.

625 g/1¼ lb fresh salmon fillet, cut into 0.5 cm/¼ in dice
1 tablespoon Dijon mustard
1 tablespoon chopped fresh dill

Salt and pepper
8 slices Sesame Brioche (see page 60) or other favourite bread

In a large stainless steel bowl, gently but thoroughly combine the salmon, mustard and dill. Liberally season with salt and pepper.

Gently form the salmon mixture into four 150 g/5 oz burgers, each 2.5 cm/1 in thick. Cover the burgers with cling film and refrigerate for at least 2 hours before using (the burgers must be refrigerated for the recommended time so they maintain their shape while cooking).

Heat a well-seasoned flat griddle or a large non-stick frying pan over a medium-high heat. When hot, cook the burgers for 3-5 minutes on each side, depending upon the preferred degree of cooking (3 minutes on each side will produce a medium-rare burger with a warm centre; 5 minutes on each side will produce a burger that is cooked through).

Toast the brioche on the griddle or in a non-stick frying pan until golden brown.

Spread each slice of the brioche with a dollop of Pernod, Mustard and Dill Mayonnaise. Serve the Salmon Burgers on the brioche immediately, each accompanied by a small ramekin of Pernod, Mustard and Dill Mayonnaise, a serving of Fennel and Red Onion Salad and lots of Sweet Potato Fries.

Pernod, Mustard and Dill Mayonnaise

Makes about 150 g/5 oz

125 g/4 oz mayonnaise
1 tablespoon Dijon mustard
1 teaspoon Pernod
½ teaspoon chopped fresh dill
Salt and pepper

In a small stainless steel bowl, whisk together the mayonnaise, mustard, Pernod and dill. Adjust the seasoning with salt and pepper and combine thoroughly. Cover with cling film and refrigerate until needed.

> *The distinct anise flavour of the Pernod in this recipe works well with the Salmon Burger and complements the Fennel and Red Onion Salad. Use the Pernod, Mustard and Dill Mayonnaise with other bold-flavoured fish dishes.*

Fennel and Red Onion Salad

Serves 4-6

3 tablespoons red wine vinegar
2 tablespoons extra-virgin olive oil
2 tablespoons sugar
1 tablespoon chopped fresh parsley
Salt and pepper
2 fennel bulbs, cored and cut into long, thin strips (see Note)
1 red onion, thinly sliced

In a large stainless steel bowl, whisk together the red wine vinegar, olive oil, sugar and parsley. Season with salt and pepper.

Toss the fennel strips and red onion slices with the dressing. Adjust the seasoning with additional salt and pepper. Cover with cling film and refrigerate for at least 2 hours before serving. The salad will keep tightly covered in the refrigerator for 2 or 3 days.

Note: Fennel is an engaging vegetable with a delicate liquorice flavour that forms a long-lasting food memory. It is now widely available, particularly during the winter months.

Cut the cored fennel bulb with a sharp stainless steel knife, or use a food processor fitted with a slicing disc.

Sweet Potato Fries

Serves 4

Vegetable oil for deep-frying
4 orange-flesh sweet potatoes, about 225 g/8 oz each, peeled
Salt and pepper

Heat the vegetable oil in a deep-fat fryer (or high-sided heavy-based saucepan) fitted with a deep-frying basket over a high heat to a temperature of 190°C/375°F.

Use a very sharp knife to slice the sweet potatoes into 0.3 cm/⅛ in thick slices. Then cut the slices into 0.3 cm/⅛ in thick strips. The potatoes may be deep-fried immediately or covered and refrigerated for up to 24 hours before frying.

Fry one-eighth of the sweet potatoes for 1½-2 minutes until lightly browned and crisp. Transfer the fried sweet potatoes to kitchen towels to drain. Repeat the frying procedure with the remaining batches of raw sweet potato strips, waiting about 45 seconds before frying each new batch to allow the oil to return to 190°C/375°F. Season with salt and pepper. Serve immediately, or keep in a warm oven for up to 30 minutes before serving.

# Provolone Ranger Burger

with Focaccia, Warm Olives and Tomatoes and Fried Mozzarella

Makes 6 burgers

Stephanie Hersh
Julia Child Productions
Cambridge, Massachusetts

SINCE HER GRADUATION FROM THE CULINARY INSTITUTE OF AMERICA, STEPHANIE HERSH HAS HELD A NUMBER OF FOOD-RELATED JOBS IN THE BOSTON AREA. STEPHANIE IS CURRENTLY WORKING ON A MASTER'S DEGREE IN LIBERAL ARTS WITH A CONCENTRATION IN GASTRONOMY AT BOSTON UNIVERSITY, RUNNING A SMALL PASTRY/CATERING BUSINESS AND TEACHING COOKING CLASSES TO PRE-SCHOOL CHILDREN AND CAKE-DECORATING CLASSES TO ADULTS. HER MOST EXCITING AND REWARDING POSITION IS AS JULIA CHILD'S FULL-TIME ASSISTANT.

STEPHANIE'S PROVOLONE RANGER BURGER WITH FRIED MOZZARELLA AND FOCACCIA DEMONSTRATES HOW SOPHISTICATED HER PALATE HAS GROWN SINCE THAT LONG-AGO SUMMER VACATION IN FLORIDA WHEN SHE AND HER FIVE COUSINS GORGED ON FAST-FOOD HAMBURGERS AT A GREAT NEW PLACE— BURGER KING. STEPHANIE NOSTALGICALLY REMEMBERS THE PROMOTIONAL SLOGAN THAT LURED HER AUNT AND UNCLE TO THIS NEW RESTAURANT: "THE BIGGER THE BURGER, THE BETTER THE BURGER; THE BURGERS ARE BIGGER AT BURGER KING"!

2 tablespoons vegetable oil
40 g/1½ oz onion, finely chopped
2 cloves garlic, finely chopped
1.1 kg/2½ lb lean minced sirloin
15 g/1 oz fresh breadcrumbs
50 g/2 oz Romano cheese, grated

1 egg, size 3, lightly beaten
1½ teaspoons salt
1 teaspoon pepper
6 slices provolone cheese
3 - 4 tablespoons olive oil

Heat the vegetable oil in a small non-stick frying pan over a medium heat. When hot, add the onions and cook for about 2 minutes until tender. Reduce the heat to low, add the garlic and cook for 1 minute. Remove the onions and garlic to a plate and place, uncovered, in the refrigerator to cool.

In a large stainless steel bowl, combine the chilled onion-garlic mixture with the minced beef. Add the breadcrumbs, Romano, egg, salt and pepper and gently but thoroughly combine.

Gently form the meat mixture into six 200 g/7 oz burgers, each 2 cm/¾ in thick. Cover the burgers with cling film and refrigerate until needed.

Grill the burgers over a medium wood or charcoal fire. Cook as desired: 3-4 minutes on each side for rare, 5-6 minutes on each side for medium and 8-9 minutes on each side for well done. Top each burger with a slice of the provolone and allow it to melt. If you have a cover for the grill, quickly melt the cheese by placing the cover over the grill for a few moments. (This burger may also be cooked on a well-seasoned flat griddle or in a large non-stick frying pan over a medium-high heat. Cook for about the same amount of time as listed for grilling.)

Remove the burgers from the grill. Brush 12 slices of Focaccia with the olive oil. Toast, oiled sides down, on the grill or griddle or in a non-stick frying pan until golden brown. Place each burger on a slice of Focaccia. Top each burger with Warm Olives and Tomatoes. Place a slice of Focaccia on top of each burger and serve with Fried Mozzarella.

Focaccia

Makes 8 slices

2 teaspoons sugar
300 ml/½ pint warm water
1 tablespoon dried yeast
400 g/14 oz plain flour
125 ml/4 fl oz olive oil
1 teaspoon salt
1 tablespoon chopped fresh basil
2 teaspoons chopped fresh oregano
½ teaspoon salt

In the bowl of an electric mixer, dissolve the sugar in 125 ml/4 fl oz of the warm water. Add the yeast and stir gently to dissolve. Allow the mixture to stand and foam for 5 minutes.

Add the flour, 50 ml/2 fl oz of the olive oil, 1 teaspoon salt and the remaining warm water. Combine on the medium speed of an electric mixer fitted with a dough hook for 2 minutes. Scrape down the sides of the bowl, then continue to mix on a low speed 5-6 minutes until the dough is smooth and elastic. If the dough forms a knot around the dough hook at any time, stop the mixer and remove the dough from the hook; continue mixing and repeat this procedure as necessary. (If a table-model electric mixer is not available, follow the directions using a hand-held mixer or kneading by hand. The mixing times will increase depending upon which alternative method is used.)

Remove the bowl from the mixer. Drizzle 1 tablespoon olive oil over the dough in the bowl and turn the dough several times to coat with the oil. Cover the bowl with a towel or cling film. Allow the dough to rise in a warm location for about 45 minutes until doubled in volume.

Preheat the oven to 200°C/400°F/Gas 6.

Lightly coat a 37.5 × 25 cm/15 × 10 in baking tray with 1 tablespoon olive oil. Line the oiled baking tray with baking parchment, then lightly coat the paper with an additional 1 tablespoon olive oil. Place the dough on to the baking tray and flatten by hand into a rectangle measuring approximately 32.5 × 22.5 cm/13 × 9 in. Brush the top of the dough with the remaining olive oil. Sprinkle the basil, oregano and salt evenly over the dough.

Bake 18-20 minutes until lightly browned.

Allow the Focaccia to cool to room temperature before cutting.

Remove the cooled Focaccia from the baking tray. Cut in half lengthways and then every 8 cm/3¼ in across the width. Cut each piece in half horizontally.

The Focaccia will keep fresh, stored in a sealed polythene bag, for 2 or 3 days at room temperature.

This bread is not only irresistible with the Provolone Ranger Burger but is also a fitting suitor to just about every burger in this book. For a light and delicious snack, try grilled Focaccia simply served with Warm Olives and Tomatoes.

Warm Olives and Tomatoes

Makes about 450 g/1 lb

50 ml/2 fl oz extra-virgin olive oil
3 cloves garlic, very finely chopped
8 fresh plum tomatoes, cored and chopped
65 g/2½ oz black olives, pitted and chopped
2 tablespoons chopped fresh basil
2 tablespoons balsamic vinegar
Salt and freshly ground black pepper

Heat the olive oil in a medium non-stick frying pan over a medium-low heat. When hot, add the garlic and cook for 1 minute. Add the plum tomatoes and continue to cook for 4 minutes. Remove from the heat and add the olives, basil and balsamic vinegar. Season with salt and pepper. Serve immediately or cool in an ice-water bath. The cooled olives and tomatoes will keep in the refrigerator for a couple of days. Heat to a simmer before serving.

A few years back, Stephanie and her cousins preferred chocolate milk shakes with their burgers. Now the beverage of choice is a glass of Pinot Noir.

Fried Mozzarella

Serves 6

450 ml/¾ pint vegetable oil
2 eggs, size 3
2 tablespoons cold water
6 × 1 cm/½ in thick slices mozzarella cheese, about 50 g/2 oz each; see Note
50 g/2 oz plain flour
175 g/6 oz dry breadcrumbs
Salt and pepper

Heat the vegetable oil in a heavy-based frying pan over a medium-high heat to a temperature of 190°C/375°F.

Whisk the eggs with the cold water until slightly foamy.

Dust the mozzarella slices with the flour and shake off any excess. Dip the slices into the beaten eggs and then into the breadcrumbs, coating them evenly, lightly and thoroughly.

Fry the cheese slices, 3 at a time, for 30 seconds on each side until golden brown and crispy. Drain the fried cheese slices on kitchen paper, season with salt and pepper and serve immediately.

Note: The mozzarella used for this recipe was cut into slices 10 cm/4 in long, 5 cm/2 in wide and 1 cm/½ in thick.

This is a somewhat hefty but nonetheless delicious meal. To lighten things up a bit, serve the burger with Fennel and Red Onion Salad (see page 79) rather than with Fried Mozzarella.

Spiced Pork Burger
with Ale and Onion Ragoût, and Carrot and Spring Onion Salad

Makes 6 burgers

James Heywood
Chef-Instructor
The Culinary Institute of America
Hyde Park, New York

WILL ANY GOOD COME FROM SPECULATING WHERE JIM HEYWOOD PICKED UP THE NICKNAME "HOG BREATH"? SUFFICE IT TO SAY THAT THIS BELOVED TEACHER REVELS IN ANY AND ALL PRESUMPTIONS AS TO THE GENESIS OF THAT MONIKER. ALTHOUGH CHEF HEYWOOD IS RENOWNED FOR HIS CHILLI RECIPE, HAVING BEEN BOTH A CONTESTANT AND A JUDGE AT SOME OF THE MOST PRESTIGIOUS CHILLI COMPETITIONS THROUGHOUT THE NATION, HIS SPICED PORK BURGER RECIPE SHOULD ENSURE THAT KUDOS COME HIS WAY.

This substantial burger should be approached with knife and fork in hand. Serve any remaining ragoût as a side dish, or save for a subsequent burger attack.

1 kg/2¼ lb trimmed fresh pork fillet, cut into 2.5 cm/1 in pieces (or 1 kg/2¼ lb minced lean pork fillet)
15 g/½ oz unsalted butter
4 tablespoons finely chopped spring onions
1 clove garlic, finely chopped
4 tablespoons chopped fresh parsley
2 teaspoons salt

1 teaspoon freshly ground black pepper
Pinch dried sage
Pinch celery seeds
Pinch ground mace
Pinch cayenne pepper
6 Onion Rolls (see page 89), cut in half
225 g/8 oz Cheddar cheese, coarsely grated

If using pork pieces, mince through a chilled meat mincer fitted with a coarse mincing plate into a large stainless steel bowl. Cover with cling film and refrigerate until needed.

Heat the butter in a small non-stick frying pan over a medium heat. When the butter has melted, add spring onions and garlic and cook for 2 minutes. Remove spring onions and garlic to a plate and place, uncovered, in the refrigerator to cool.

Combine the chilled spring onion and garlic mixture with the minced pork. Add the parsley, salt, ground black pepper, sage, celery seeds, mace and cayenne pepper. Gently but thoroughly combine the ingredients.

Gently form the meat mixture into six 175 g/6 oz burgers, each 2.5 cm/1 in thick. Cover the burgers with cling film and refrigerate until needed.

Preheat the oven to 150°C/300°F/Gas 2.

Heat a well-seasoned flat griddle or a large non-stick frying pan over a medium heat. When hot, cook the burgers for 2-3 minutes on each side. Place the burgers on a baking sheet in the oven for 15-16 minutes until medium. Remove the burgers from the oven.

Toast the rolls, cut sides down, on the griddle or a non-stick frying pan over a medium-high heat until golden brown.

Portion 2 tablespoons hot Ale and Onion Ragoût on to the bottom half of each toasted roll. Place a burger on each ragoût-covered roll. Evenly divide the Cheddar over the burgers. Top with the other halves of the toasted rolls and serve immediately with Carrot and Spring Onion Salad.

Chef Heywood is also fond of using this savoury ragoût with pan-fried veal cutlets.

Ale and Onion Ragoût

Serves 6

25 g/1 oz unsalted butter
2 teaspoons paprika
2 onions, sliced 0.3 cm/^{1}/$_8$ in thick
2 cloves garlic, very finely chopped
5 tablespoons plain flour
125 ml/4 fl oz chicken stock, hot
3 tablespoons ketchup
1 tablespoon coarse whole-grain mustard
350 ml/12 fl oz ale or beer
Salt and pepper

Melt the butter in a large saucepan over a medium-high heat. When hot, add the paprika and constantly stir for 2 minutes. Add the onions and garlic and cook, stirring frequently, for 10-12 minutes until the onions are translucent. Reduce the heat to medium.

Add the flour and cook for 3-4 minutes, stirring constantly to prevent browning or scorching.

Add the hot chicken stock, ketchup and mustard. Stir the mixture constantly for 6-8 minutes until thickened and smooth.

Add the ale or beer and stir to incorporate. Bring the ragoût to the boil, then lower the heat and allow to simmer for 15-20 minutes. Adjust the seasoning with salt and pepper.

Serve Ale and Onion Ragoût hot over Spiced Pork Burgers.

This ragoût may be cooled in an ice-water bath, then stored covered in the refrigerator for several days. Heat the ragoût to a boil before serving.

Carrot and Spring Onion Salad

Serves 6

1^1/$_2$ teaspoons salt
900 g/2 lb carrots, peeled and trimmed
50 ml/2 fl oz distilled white vinegar
6 tablespoons vegetable oil
^{1}/$_2$ tablespoon prepared Creole mustard (see Note)
^{1}/$_2$ tablespoon clear honey
^{1}/$_2$ tablespoon chopped fresh dill
^{1}/$_2$ tablespoon chopped fresh parsley
^{1}/$_2$ teaspoon white pepper
6 spring onions, trimmed and thinly sliced diagonally

Bring a large saucepan of water and 1 teaspoon salt to the boil over high heat. Cook the carrots in the boiling water for 14-15 minutes until tender. Drain the carrots, then plunge them into ice water. When the carrots are thoroughly cooled, remove from the ice water and drain well. Cut the cooled carrots into 0.3 cm/^{1}/$_8$ in thick diagonal slices.

In a large stainless steel bowl, whisk together the white vinegar, vegetable oil, mustard, honey, dill and parsley. Add the remaining ^{1}/$_2$ teaspoon salt and the pepper and combine thoroughly. Add the carrots and spring onions and toss gently to combine. The salad can be kept tightly covered in a non-metallic container in the refrigerator for 3 or 4 days.

Note: If Creole mustard is not available, use your favourite spicy mustard.

Veal and Smoked Gouda Burger
with Creamy Mustard Dill Potato Salad

Makes 6 burgers

Liz Heywood

Chef-Instructor
The Culinary Institute of America
Hyde Park, New York

CHEF LIZ HEYWOOD DID NOT VENTURE
FAR FROM THE INSTITUTE FOLLOWING
GRADUATION. RATHER, SHE CHOSE TO DO
A FELLOWSHIP (IN EFFECT TO BECOME A
TEACHER'S ASSISTANT) IN THE HIGHLY
TOUTED ESCOFFIER RESTAURANT AT
THE INSTITUTE. SHE THEN WORKED AS
SOUS CHEF AT THE BEEKMAN ARMS IN
RHINEBECK, NEW YORK, UNTIL 1978,
WHEN SHE STARTED COUNTRY BUFFET,
A CATERING AND SPECIALITY BAKING
OPERATION.

LIZ IS PRESENTLY A CHEF-INSTRUCTOR
AT THE CULINARY INSTITUTE, AND SHE IS
STILL RUNNING THE CATERING BUSINESS
IN HER SPARE TIME.

LIZ'S VEAL AND SMOKED GOUDA BURGER
CARRIES THE SAME COUNTRY FLAIR THAT
IS A TRADEMARK OF HER CATERING FIRM.

---

*The absence of a sauce or condiment
to dress the burger may tempt one to
reach for a ketchup bottle. Although
this is not* verboten, *it is not
encouraged, since the cheese and the
potato salad provide a creamy contrast
for this already juicy burger.*

---

1 tablespoon olive oil
65 g/2½ oz onion, finely diced
1 green apple, such as Granny Smith
1 teaspoon finely chopped garlic
4 tablespoons chopped fresh parsley
2 teaspoons salt
1 teaspoon chopped fresh oregano
1 teaspoon chopped fresh sage
¾ teaspoon freshly ground black pepper
750 g/1½ lb minced veal
125 g/4 oz pork fat, diced
6 slices smoked Gouda cheese (see Note)
6 Onion Rolls (see page 89), cut in half
1 large bunch watercress, stalks trimmed, washed and dried

Heat the olive oil in a medium non-stick frying pan over a medium heat. When hot, add the onions and cook for 10 minutes until lightly browned. While the onions are cooking, core and dice the apple (do not peel). Add the diced apple and garlic to the lightly browned onions and cook for 2 minutes. Add the parsley, salt, oregano, sage and pepper and stir to combine. Transfer onion-apple mixture to a plate and place, uncovered, in refrigerator to cool.

In a large stainless steel bowl, gently but thoroughly combine the minced veal, cooled onion-apple mixture and pork fat.

Gently form the meat mixture into six 175 g/6 oz burgers, each 2.5 cm/1 in thick. Cover with cling film and refrigerate until needed.

Preheat the oven to 160°C/325°F/Gas 2.

Heat a well-seasoned flat griddle or a large non-stick frying pan over a medium-high heat. When hot, cook the burgers for 2 minutes on each side. Transfer burgers to a baking tray and finish cooking in the oven: 8-10 minutes for medium and 10-12 minutes for medium-well done. Remove burgers from oven and top each with a slice of Gouda.

Toast the roll halves on the griddle or in a non-stick frying pan over a medium-high heat until golden brown. Serve the Veal and Smoked Gouda Burgers immediately on the toasted buns accompanied by Creamy Mustard Dill Potato Salad and garnished with the watercress sprigs.

Note: If smoked gouda is not available, substitute another mild-flavoured smoked cheese.

Creamy Mustard Dill Potato Salad

Serves 6

1.1 kg/2½ lb potatoes, preferably red-skinned, washed but not peeled
Salt and pepper
1 tablespoon mustard seeds
4 tablespoons red wine vinegar
2 tablespoons Dijon mustard
1 tablespoon mayonnaise
2 tablespoons chopped fresh dill
1 tablespoon chopped fresh parsley
1 tablespoon spring onions, finely chopped
1 clove garlic, finely chopped
1 teaspoon sugar
¼ teaspoon Worcestershire sauce
225 ml/8 fl oz safflower or vegetable oil
125 ml/4 fl oz extra-virgin olive oil

Place the potatoes in a large saucepan and cover with cold water. Bring to a simmer over a medium-high heat, then adjust the heat and allow to simmer slowly for 20-22 minutes until potatoes are tender. Drain the hot water from the potatoes, then cool under slowly running cold water until cool to the touch. Refrigerate the potatoes for 30 minutes. Slice the chilled potatoes into 0.5 cm/¼ in thick slices. Lightly season the sliced potatoes with salt and pepper.

Preheat the oven to 190°C/375°F/Gas 5.

Toast the mustard seeds on a baking tray in the oven for 2 minutes. Allow to cool.

Prepare the dressing in a large stainless steel bowl by whisking together the red wine vinegar, mustard and mayonnaise. Add the dill, parsley, spring onions, garlic, sugar, Worcestershire sauce and toasted mustard seeds. Continue to whisk the mixture while adding a slow, steady stream of the safflower or vegetable oil, then the olive oil. Adjust the seasoning with salt and pepper and combine thoroughly.

Gently toss the potato slices with the dressing. Cover the bowl with cling film and refrigerate for 2-3 hours before serving. The salad will keep covered in the refrigerator for 2 days.

> *This salad is liberally dressed intentionally. For a lighter salad, the dressing recipe may be cut in half, resulting in a less viscous yet still pleasing potato salad.*

Sally's Famous Hamburger
with Onion Rolls

Makes 4 burgers

Gerry Klaskala
Chef/Managing Partner
The Buckhead Diner
Atlanta, Georgia

ARGUABLY ATLANTA'S MOST POPULAR
RESTAURANT, THE BUCKHEAD DINER
ALMOST ALWAYS HAS A CLUSTER OF
HUNGRY PATRONS WAITING TO BE SEATED.
THIS IS DUE TO THE FACT THAT GERRY
KLASKALA IS AHEAD OF HIS COMPETITION
IN THAT MAGIC COMBINATION OF
EDUCATION, TRAINING, CREATIVITY AND
SKILLS, WHICH ENABLES HIM TO PREPARE
THE DELICIOUS FOOD HIS CUSTOMERS
HAVE COME TO EXPECT.

HOWEVER, AFTER A HARD WEEK AT THE
DINER, GERRY IS LIKELY TO BE FOUND
RELAXING WHILE HIS WIFE, SALLY, DOES
THE COOKING. ALTHOUGH SALLY IS NOT
AN ALUMNA OF THE INSTITUTE, SHE
PRIDES HERSELF ON MAKING A GREAT
HAMBURGER.

PROFESSIONALLY SPEAKING, THESE
BURGERS ARE DELICIOUS.

---

*Gerry encourages you to embellish
Sally's burger with a slice or two of
your favourite cheese. Also de rigueur
with burgers at Gerry and Sally's
house is a bottle of ketchup and a jar
of horseradish mustard.*

---

750 g/1½ lb minced beef
150 g/5 oz onions, finely
  chopped
50 g/2 oz dry breadcrumbs
1 egg, size 3, lightly beaten
1 tablespoon prepared
  mustard
2 teaspoons Worcestershire
  sauce
1 teaspoon horseradish sauce

1 teaspoon chopped fresh
  oregano
Salt and pepper to season
4 tablespoons mayonnaise
4 iceberg lettuce leaves,
  washed and dried
Spiced Tomato Relish
(see page 38)

In a large stainless steel bowl, place the minced beef, onions, breadcrumbs, egg, mustard, Worcestershire sauce, horseradish and oregano. Season with salt and pepper and gently but thoroughly combine.

Gently form the mixture into four 225 g/8 oz burgers, each 3 cm/1¼ in thick. Cover the burgers with cling film and refrigerate until needed.

Grill the burgers over a medium wood or charcoal fire. Cook as desired: 4-5 minutes on each side for rare, 6-7 minutes on each side for medium and 9-10 minutes on each side for well done. (This burger may also be cooked on a well-seasoned flat griddle or in a large non-stick frying pan over a medium-high heat. Cook for about the same amount of time as listed for grilling.)

Cut 4 Onion Rolls in half. Toast the Onion Rolls, cut sides down, on the grill or griddle or in a non-stick frying pan until golden brown.

Spread the top half of each roll with 1 tablespoon mayonnaise. Place a burger on the bottom half of each toasted roll. Top each burger with 1 of the lettuce leaves, 1-2 tablespoons Spiced Tomato Relish and a top roll half.

Onion Rolls

Makes 12 rolls

**50 ml/2 fl oz olive oil, plus 2 tablespoons and
1 teaspoon**
450 g/1 lb onions, thinly sliced
2½ teaspoons salt
¼ teaspoon cracked black pepper
1 tablespoon sugar
400 ml/14 fl oz warm water
2 tablespoons dried yeast
800 g/26 oz plain flour

Heat 50 ml/2 fl oz olive oil in a saucepan over a medium heat. When hot, add the onions, ½ teaspoon salt and pepper. Cover the pan and cook for 10 minutes until the onions are translucent. Transfer the onions to a plate and leave, uncovered, at room temperature until needed.

In the bowl of an electric mixer, dissolve the sugar in 125 ml/4 fl oz warm water. Add the yeast and stir gently to dissolve. Allow the mixture to stand and foam for 5-6 minutes.

Place the mixing bowl on an electric mixer fitted with a dough hook. On top of the yeast mixture, add 750 g/ 1½ lb of the flour, the remaining warm water, 65 g/2½ oz cooked onions, 2 tablespoons olive oil and the remaining 2 teaspoons salt. Mix on a low speed for 1 minute, then scrape down the sides of the bowl. Continue to mix on a low speed for an additional minute, then scrape down the sides of the bowl. Adjust the mixer speed to medium-low and mix for 3-4 minutes until the dough is smooth and elastic. (If a table-model electric mixer is not available, follow the directions using a hand-held mixer or kneading by hand. The mixing times will increase depending upon which alternative method is used.)

Remove the bowl from the mixer. Drizzle the remaining 1 teaspoon olive oil over the dough in the bowl and turn the dough several times to coat with the oil. Cover the dough with a towel or cling film. Allow the dough to rise in a warm location about 45 minutes until doubled in size.

Preheat the oven to 160°C/325°F/Gas 3.

When the dough has doubled in size, knock it back to its original size. Once again cover with a towel or cling film and allow to double in size for a second time, which will take about 30 minutes.

Place the dough on a clean, lightly floured work surface, using the remaining flour as necessary. Use a sharp knife to cut the dough into 12 equal portions. Shape each portion of dough into a smooth ball. Place the dough balls on to 2 baking trays lined with baking parchment. Loosely cover each baking tray of rolls with cling film. Allow the rolls to rise in a warm location for 35-40 minutes until doubled in size. Slightly flatten the top of each roll using your fingertips. Equally divide the remaining cooked onions on to the rolls, spreading evenly over the tops. Bake the rolls 35-40 minutes until they are golden in colour and the onions are caramelised.

Allow the rolls to cool thoroughly before slicing them horizontally.

The rolls will keep fresh for 2 or 3 days at room temperature stored in a sealed polythene bag.

These versatile rolls not only will complement virtually every burger in this book, they also are terrific for sandwiches. Try your favourite sandwich filling on Gerry's Onion Roll— and you may just find yourself baking as many as they do at The Buckhead Diner—well, almost!

Hamburger à la Lindstrom

with Mounds of Golden Crisp-fried Onions and Dilled Soured Cream

Makes 4 burgers

Jenifer Lang
Managing Director/Owner
Café des Artistes
New York, New York

A SELF-PROCLAIMED "FOOD FREAK" AS WELL AS AN ACCOMPLISHED JOURNALIST, JENIFER LANG ENROLLED AT THE CULINARY INSTITUTE IN ORDER TO ENHANCE HER SKILLS WITH A PROFESSIONAL CHEF'S TRAINING.

AFTER GRADUATING FROM THE INSTITUTE, JENIFER BECAME CHEF AT NATHANS IN GEORGETOWN. SINCE 1990, SHE HAS BEEN THE MANAGING DIRECTOR OF THE THREE-STAR CAFÉ DES ARTISTES. JENIFER CONTINUES TO WRITE, AND SHE MAKES FREQUENT APPEARANCES ON NATIONAL TELEVISION. HER ARTICLES ON FOOD, RESTAURANTS AND CONSUMER SUBJECTS APPEAR IN MANY NATIONAL FOOD AND GENERAL-INTEREST MAGAZINES.

THIS SCANDINAVIAN-INSPIRED HAMBURGER À LA LINDSTROM IS A MEAL IN ITSELF, WITH MEAT, POTATO AND VEGETABLE ALL TOGETHER. JENIFER ORIGINALLY DEVISED IT FOR HER SON, SIMON, AS A WAY TO SNEAK VEGETABLES INTO HIS BURGERS.

15 g/½ oz unsalted butter
40 g/1½ oz onion, finely chopped
65 g/2½ oz fresh beetroot, peeled and diced
2 teaspoons salt
65 g/2½ oz potatoes, peeled and diced

625 g/1¼ lb lean minced beef
Salt and freshly ground black pepper
4 Onion Rolls (see page 89) or other favourite rolls, cut in half

Melt the butter in a small non-stick frying pan over a medium-high heat. When the butter is hot, cook the onions for 2-3 minutes until tender. Transfer the onions to a plate and place, uncovered, in the refrigerator to cool.

In a large saucepan, cover the beetroot with water with 1 teaspoon salt. Cook over a medium-high heat, bringing the water to the simmer. Adjust the heat and continue to simmer slowly for 10-15 minutes until the beetroot is thoroughly cooked yet still firm. Drain the cooked beetroot, then transfer to a plate and cool, uncovered, in the refrigerator.

In a large saucepan, cover the potatoes with water salted with the remaining salt. Cook over a medium-high heat, bringing the water to the simmer. Adjust the heat and continue to simmer slowly for 7-8 minutes until the potatoes are cooked but still firm. Drain the cooked potatoes, then transfer to a plate and cool, uncovered, in the refrigerator.

In a stainless steel bowl, gently but thoroughly combine the minced beef, onions, beetroot and potatoes.

Gently form the minced beef mixture into four 200 g/7 oz burgers, each 2.5 cm/1 in thick. Season with salt and pepper. Cover the burgers with cling film and refrigerate until needed.

Heat a well-seasoned flat griddle or a large non-stick frying pan over a medium-high heat. When hot, cook the burgers for 3-4 minutes on each side for rare, 5-6 minutes on each side for medium and 8-9 minutes on each side for well done.

Toast the roll halves, cut sides down, on the griddle or in a non-stick frying pan until golden brown.

Serve each burger, topped with 1-2 tablespoons Dilled Soured Cream, on a toasted roll accompanied by Mounds of Golden Crisp-fried Onions.

Mounds of Golden Crisp-fried Onions

Serves 4

Vegetable oil for deep-frying
175 g/6 oz plain flour
2 tablespoons freshly ground black pepper
2 teaspoons salt
2 large onions, halved and thinly sliced
Salt and pepper

Heat the vegetable oil in a deep-fat fryer (or high-sided, heavy-based saucepan) over a high heat to a temperature of 180°C/350°F.

In a large stainless steel bowl, thoroughly combine the flour, freshly ground black pepper and 2 teaspoons salt.

Toss the sliced onions in the seasoned flour. Coat the onions evenly, lightly and thoroughly. Shake off excess flour.

Fry a quarter of the onions for about 2 minutes until golden brown and crispy. Use a skimmer or a large slotted spoon to transfer the fried onions to kitchen towels to drain. Repeat the frying procedure with the remaining

batches of onions, waiting about 2 minutes before frying each new batch to allow the oil to return to 180°C/350°F. Season with salt and pepper. Serve immediately.

The onions will keep warm and crispy in a warm oven for up to 30 minutes.

Dilled Soured Cream

Makes 125 ml/4 fl oz

125 ml/4 fl oz soured cream
2 tablespoons minced red onions
1 teaspoon chopped fresh dill
Salt and pepper

In a small stainless steel bowl, combine the soured cream, red onions and dill and blend the mixture together. Adjust the seasoning with salt and pepper, and combine thoroughly. Serve immediately, or keep tightly covered in the refrigerator for 2 or 3 days.

Lentil Walnut Burger

with Ginger Yogurt Dressing, Vinegar Greens and Basmati Rice with Vegetable Confetti

Makes 6 burgers

Daniel Leader
Owner/Baker
Bread Alone
Boiceville, New York

BUILDING A WOOD-FIRED BRICK OVEN WAS NOT PART OF THE CURRICULUM AT THE CULINARY INSTITUTE WHEN DAN LEADER WAS THERE. BUT EVEN THEN, HE HAD A PASSION FOR BREAD-BAKING—SPECIFICALLY TRADITIONAL EUROPEAN HEARTH-BAKED BREADS. SO FOLLOWING GRADUATION, DAN TRAVELLED EXTENSIVELY IN EUROPE, STUDYING TRADITIONAL METHODS OF BREAD-BAKING AND LEARNING TO BUILD A WOOD-FIRED BRICK OVEN. AT BREAD ALONE, DAN HAS WOOD-FIRED BRICK OVENS THAT HE BUILT HIMSELF.

DAN LEADER'S BURGER IS EXEMPLARY OF THE WHOLESOME APPROACH HE TAKES TO LIFE AND HIS CRAFT.

French green lentils, specifically those labelled La Lentille Verte du Puy, *simply have no peers. These fine little beans have delicate skins, a firm texture and a nutty flavour. Grown in volcanic-enriched soil, they are loaded with nutritionally beneficial components and are worth their price.*

300 g/10 oz Puy green lentils, picked over, washed and drained
2 teaspoons salt
3 tablespoons safflower or vegetable oil
65 g/2½ oz onions, finely chopped
2 teaspoons finely chopped garlic
1 teaspoon grated fresh ginger
75 g/3 oz chopped walnuts, toasted
Salt and pepper
6 wholemeal pitta breads

Place the lentils in a large saucepan, cover with cold water and 2 teaspoons salt and bring to the simmer. Adjust the heat to simmer the lentils slowly for 20–25 minutes until soft. Drain the cooked lentils in a colander. Transfer the lentils to a large plate or platter and keep, uncovered, in the refrigerator to cool.

Heat 1 tablespoon safflower or vegetable oil in a small non-stick frying pan over a medium-high heat. When hot, add the onions, garlic and ginger and cook for 2-3 minutes until tender. Transfer the onion mixture to a plate and place, uncovered, in the refrigerator to cool.

Purée 50 g/2 oz of the walnuts in a food processor fitted with a metal blade.

In a large stainless steel bowl, gently but thoroughly combine the cooled lentils, chilled onion mixture, remaining walnuts and walnut purée. Season with salt and pepper.

Form lentil mixture into six 150 g/5 oz burgers, each 2 cm/³/4 in thick. Cover with cling film and refrigerate until needed.

Preheat the oven to 180°C/350°F/Gas 4.

Heat the remaining 2 tablespoons safflower or vegetable oil in a large non-stick frying pan over a medium-high heat. When hot, cook the burgers about 2 minutes on each side until lightly browned. Transfer the burgers to a baking tray and place in the oven for 8-10 minutes. About 1 or 2 minutes before burgers are finished cooking, place the pitta breads on a baking tray in the oven to warm.

Remove the pitta breads and burgers from the oven. Cut a slice from the top of each pitta bread and gently split open the bread. Stuff each pitta with a Lentil Walnut Burger and spoon 2-3 teaspoons Ginger Yogurt Dressing directly on the meat. Serve burgers accompanied by Vinegar Greens and Basmati Rice with Vegetable Confetti.

Ginger Yogurt Dressing

Makes 225 ml/8 fl oz

225 g/8 oz low-fat plain yogurt
1 tablespoon grated fresh ginger
1 teaspoon chopped fresh parsley
Salt and pepper

In a small stainless steel bowl, combine the yogurt, ginger and parsley. Season with salt and pepper, then combine thoroughly. Serve immediately, or refrigerate tightly covered for up to 3-4 hours before serving.

Vinegar Greens

Serves 6

2 tablespoons safflower or vegetable oil
2 tablespoons water
3 bunches Swiss or ruby chard, stalks removed, washed, dried and torn into 5-7.5 cm/2-3 in pieces (see Note)
1 tablespoon balsamic vinegar
Freshly ground black pepper

Heat the safflower or vegetable oil and water in a large non-stick frying pan over a medium-high heat. When hot, add the chard. Steam the greens for 3-4 minutes until hot and wilted. Remove from the heat and finish by splashing the chard with the balsamic vinegar and with a grind or two of pepper. Serve immediately.

Note: If chard is not available, use whatever seasonal greens look fresh and salubrious, such as spinach, curly kale or collard greens.

The flavour of this dressing is at its peak when freshly prepared. Dan suggests that you prepare it as close to serving time as possible. Dan also makes a point of using fresh ginger, since its pure, spicy flavour simply has no substitute.

Basmati Rice with Vegetable Confetti

Serves 6

2 tablespoons olive oil
125 g/4 oz carrot, finely diced
125 g/4 oz red onion, finely diced
50 g/2 oz celery, finely diced
50 g/2 oz red pepper, finely diced
Salt and white pepper
300 g/10 oz white basmati rice
750 ml/1¼ pints water or vegetable stock, hot

Heat the olive oil in a large saucepan over a medium-high heat. When hot, add the carrot, red onion, celery and red pepper. Season with salt and pepper and cook for 4-5 minutes. Add the rice and stir to combine thoroughly. Then add the hot water or vegetable stock. Adjust the heat to high and bring to the boil. As soon as the liquid boils, cover the saucepan and reduce the heat to medium. Allow the rice to cook undisturbed for 12-15 minutes until tender. Remove the saucepan from the heat. Serve the rice immediately, or keep, covered, away from the heat, for up to 45 minutes.

Veal and Apricot Burger
with Honey Mustard Cream and
Apple and Walnut Salad

Makes 4 burgers

Vinnie Oakes

*Vice President of Food and Beverage
Desert Inn Hotel and Country Club
Las Vegas, Nevada*

WHEN HE GRADUATED FROM THE
CULINARY INSTITUTE OF AMERICA, VINNIE
OAKES KNEW THAT HIS FOOD-SERVICE
CAREER WOULD TAKE HIM BEYOND
THE KITCHEN. TO PREPARE FOR THE
OPPORTUNITIES IN MANAGEMENT, VINNIE
ATTENDED THE UNIVERSITY OF DENVER,
MAJORING IN HOTEL AND RESTAURANT
MANAGEMENT. HE GRADUATED IN 1969
WITH A BACHELOR OF SCIENCE DEGREE
IN BUSINESS ADMINISTRATION.

AFTER GRADUATION FROM THE
UNIVERSITY OF DENVER, VINNIE WORKED
FOR THE LEGENDARY GEORGE LANG
AT RESTAURANT ASSOCIATES. HE LATER
JOINED HARRAH'S HOTEL AND CASINO AS
DIRECTOR OF FOOD OPERATIONS AND
THEN BECAME DIRECTOR OF THE FOOD
DIVISION FOR SILVER DOLLAR CITY THEME
PARK IN BRANSON, MISSOURI. VINNIE IS
PRESENTLY VICE PRESIDENT OF FOOD AND
BEVERAGE AT THE DESERT INN HOTEL
AND COUNTRY CLUB IN LAS VEGAS.

VINNIE'S BURGER IS PROOF THAT YOU
CAN TAKE A CULINARY GRADUATE OUT
OF THE KITCHEN BUT YOU CANNOT TAKE
THE KITCHEN OUT OF HIS PSYCHE. VINNIE
BASED THIS BURGER ON THE TRADITIONAL
DANISH MEAT PATTY CALLED *FRIKADELLER*.

350 g/12 oz lean veal, cut into
2.5 cm/1 in pieces (or 350 g/
12 oz minced lean veal)

225 g/8 oz trimmed pork fillet,
cut into 2.5 cm/1 in pieces
(or 225 g/8 oz minced
trimmed pork fillet)

65 g/2½ onion, finely chopped

25 g/1 oz dried apricots, finely
chopped

1 teaspoon salt

½ teaspoon white pepper

¼ teaspoon finely chopped
fresh rosemary

8 slices rye bread

If using veal and pork pieces, mince through a meat mincer fitted with a
coarse mincing plate into a large stainless steel bowl.

Add the onions, apricots, salt, pepper and rosemary to the minced meats.
Gently but thoroughly combine the ingredients.

Gently form the veal-pork mixture into four 175 g/6 oz burgers, each
2.5 cm/1 in thick. Cover the burgers with cling film and refrigerate until
needed.

Preheat the oven to 190°C/375°F/Gas 5.

Heat a well-seasoned flat griddle or large non-stick frying pan over a
medium-high heat. When hot, sear the burgers for 2 minutes on each side
until golden brown. Transfer the burgers to a baking tray and finish cooking
in the oven for 10-12 minutes.

Toast the rye bread in the oven or in a toaster just prior to removing the
burgers from the oven.

Spread the toasted bread slices with Honey Mustard Cream. Serve each
Veal and Apricot Burger between 2 slices of the bread, and accompany the
burgers with Apple and Walnut Salad.

Honey Mustard Cream

Makes about 150 ml/5 fl oz

125 ml/4 fl oz soured cream
2 tablespoons Dijon mustard
1 tablespoon honey
Salt and pepper

In a small stainless steel bowl, combine the soured cream, mustard and honey. Adjust the seasoning with salt and pepper and combine thoroughly. The Honey Mustard Cream can be stored tightly covered in a non-corrosive container in the refrigerator for up to 1 week.

As none of the Scandinavian countries produce grape wines, it would seem natural to suggest a glass of golden beer to accompany this Danish-inspired burger. If you want to become totally immersed in the Scandinavian spirit, try pairing a beer with a very cold shot of Aquavit.

Apple and Walnut Salad

Serves 4

125 g/4 oz mayonnaise
¼ teaspoon finely chopped fresh rosemary
Salt and pepper
2 Red Delicious apples, washed
75 g/3 oz celery, sliced diagonally
40 g/1½ oz dried apricots, diced
50 g/2 oz walnuts, toasted

In a large stainless steel bowl, combine the mayonnaise and rosemary. Adjust the seasoning with salt and pepper and combine thoroughly.

Core and dice the apples into 1 cm/½ in pieces (do not peel). Toss the apples, celery, apricots and walnuts with the dressing to coat lightly but thoroughly. Serve immediately. The Apple and Walnut Salad will keep tightly covered in the refrigerator for several hours (without the apples discolouring).

This salad was obviously inspired by the traditional Waldorf salad. However, in Vinnie's version, the addition of fresh rosemary and dried apricots gives the recipe a culinarian's innovative touch.

 # Beef Sirloin and Kidney Burger
with Grain-Mustard Butter and Steamed Asparagus

Makes 4 burgers

Charles Palmer
Executive Chef/Owner
Aureole
New York, New York

LEAVE IT TO CHARLES PALMER, WHO HAS
NO QUALMS ABOUT TANTALISING THE
TASTE BUDS WITH HIS SPECIAL BRAND
OF CUISINE AT THE ELEGANT AUREOLE
RESTAURANT, TO DEVISE AN ELEGANT
SIRLOIN BURGER THAT GETS A GREAT BIG
BOOST OF FLAVOUR FROM FRESH BEEF
KIDNEYS.

  CHARLES' BEEF SIRLOIN AND KIDNEY
BURGER REFLECTS HIS POLICY OF
RETAINING THE TRUE AND HONEST
FLAVOUR OF FOOD—YET THROWING IN
AN ELEMENT OF SURPRISE.

Charles recommends that a good
fragrant dark ale be enjoyed with his
burger. He also suggests that his Beef
Sirloin and Kidney Burgers would be
equally delicious served on sourdough
rolls or bread.

- 625 g/1¼ lb lean sirloin, cut into 2.5 cm/1 in cubes (or 625 g/1¼ lb minced lean beef sirloin)
- 225 g/8 oz beef kidneys, trimmed of fat and membrane and cut into 2.5 cm/1 in cubes (or 175 g/6 oz minced beef kidneys; see Note)
- 4 tablespoons extra-virgin olive oil
- 4 tablespoons finely chopped spring onions
- ¼ teaspoon salt
- ½ teaspoon coarsely ground black pepper
- 25 g/1 oz unsalted butter
- 2 large onions, thinly sliced Salt and pepper
- 225 ml/8 fl oz chicken stock
- 4 Onion Rolls (see page 89), cut in half

If using beef and kidney cubes, mince through a meat mincer fitted with a coarse mincing plate into a large stainless steel bowl.

Gently but thoroughly combine the ground meats with 3 tablespoons olive oil, spring onions, salt and coarsely ground black pepper.

Gently form the sirloin-kidney mixture into four 200 g/7 oz burgers, each 2.5 cm/1 in thick. Cover the burgers with cling film and refrigerate until needed.

Heat the butter in a large non-stick frying pan over a medium heat. When melted, add the onions, salt and pepper and cook 25-30 minutes until caramelised. Add the chicken stock and bring to the boil. Lower the heat and simmer very slowly for 15 minutes. The caramelised onions may be kept warm while preparing the remainder of the recipe, or they can be cooled, refrigerated and re-heated when needed.

Prior to grilling, brush the burgers with the remaining 1 tablespoon olive oil.

Grill the burgers over a medium wood or charcoal fire. Cook as desired: 3-4 minutes on each side for rare, 5-6 minutes on each side for medium and 8-9 minutes on each side for well done. (This burger may also be cooked on a well-seasoned flat griddle or in a large non-stick frying pan over a medium-high heat. Cook for about the same amount of time as listed for grilling.)

Toast the rolls, cut sides down, on the grill or griddle or in a non-stick frying pan until golden brown. Spread the toasted rolls with Grain-Mustard Butter. Serve the burgers on the rolls with the warm caramelised onions, accompanied by Steamed Asparagus.

Note: Kidneys can be found in most major supermarkets. A fresh beef kidney will have a clean, although slightly acidic, smell. Avoid purchasing kidneys that have lost their bright red colour or that have an aroma that makes you wrinkle your nose.

Grain-Mustard Butter

Makes about 150 g/5 oz

125 g/4 oz unsalted butter, softened
2 tablespoons coarse whole-grain mustard
¹/₂ teaspoon fresh lemon juice
¹/₂ teaspoon salt
¹/₂ teaspoon freshly ground black pepper

In a small stainless steel bowl, combine the butter and mustard and stir until smooth. Add the lemon juice, salt and pepper and stir until the lemon juice is incorporated. The butter can be stored, covered, in the refrigerator for several days.

Steamed Asparagus

Serves 4

25 g/1 oz unsalted butter
Finely grated rind of 1 lemon
¹/₂ teaspoon cracked black pepper
750 g/1¹/₂ lb asparagus
¹/₂ teaspoon salt

In a small stainless steel bowl, combine the butter, lemon rind and pepper. Set aside at room temperature until needed.

Snap the woody end from each stalk of the asparagus. Lightly peel the asparagus and cut each stalk diagonally into 2.5 cm/1 in pieces.

Heat 50 ml/2 fl oz water and the salt in a large non-stick frying pan over a high heat. When the water begins to boil, add the asparagus pieces and steam for 3-4 minutes until tender and bright green. Remove the pan from the heat and add the lemon butter. Toss lightly to coat the asparagus pieces. Serve immediately.

Wisconsin Campfire Burger

with Beer and Cheese Bread and Pan-fried New Potatoes

Makes 4 burgers

Jon Pierre Peavey
Assistant Chef
The Trellis Restaurant
Williamsburg, Virginia

MUCH OF WHAT JON PIERRE PEAVEY KNEW ABOUT COOKING BEFORE COMING TO THE CULINARY INSTITUTE OF AMERICA CAME THE OLD-FASHIONED WAY—HE LEARNED IT FROM HIS FATHER.

JON PIERRE'S DAD WAS A MASTER OF CAMPFIRE CUISINE—NOT ENTIRELY UNUSUAL FOR ONE WHO HAILS FROM INDIANHEAD COUNTRY, A.K.A. EAU CLAIRE, WISCONSIN. AS A CHILD, JON PIERRE ENJOYED MANY FISHING AND CAMPING TRIPS WITH HIS FAMILY, AND HE HAS FOND MEMORIES OF HIS FATHER'S OUTDOOR PROWESS. MR PEAVEY ALWAYS SAID HE COULD SURVIVE IN THE WOODS WITH ONLY A HATCHET, A TRAPPER'S BLANKET, AND A POUND OF SALT. THE FACT IS THAT MR PEAVEY ALSO HAD A SUBSTANTIAL INVENTORY OF CAMPING EQUIPMENT, INCLUDING A RATHER ONEROUS BUT INVALUABLE IRON FRYING PAN. BLACK AND SOOTY, THIS PAN WAS FONDLY REFERRED TO AS "WELL SEASONED"; IT WAS ALWAYS CLEANED BY RUBBING IT WITH BACON GREASE, THEN TURNING IT UPSIDE DOWN OVER THE DYING EMBERS OF THE DAY'S CAMPFIRE. JON PIERRE INHERITED THIS PAN UNDER THE CONDITION THAT IT NEVER BE WASHED WITH ANYTHING AS ODIOUS AS SOAP.

JON PIERRE ALSO INHERITED HIS FATHER'S PASSION FOR DELICIOUS FOOD, AND HIS WISCONSIN CAMPFIRE BURGER WOULD MAKE HIS LATE FATHER PROUD.

900 g/2 lb fresh minced beef
1 bunch spring onions, trimmed and thinly sliced diagonally
5 tablespoons beer
2 teaspoons salt
1 teaspoon freshly ground black pepper
350 g/12 oz mushrooms, stalks trimmed and thinly sliced

In a large stainless steel bowl, gently but thoroughly combine the minced beef, spring onions, beer, salt and pepper.

Gently form the meat mixture into four 225 g/8 oz burgers, each 3 cm/1¼ in thick. Cover the burgers with cling film and refrigerate until needed.

Cut four 45 × 30 cm/18 × 12 in sheets of aluminium foil. Place one-quarter of the mushrooms in the middle of each sheet of foil. Place a burger on top of each portion of mushrooms. Bring 2 edges of the foil together and roll the foil down to the top of the burger. Twist each end to form a handle. Keep the burgers well chilled until a few moments before cooking.

Cook the burgers directly on the coals of a low wood or charcoal fire. Cook as desired: 5 minutes on each side for rare, 7 minutes on each side for medium and 9 minutes on each side for well done.

Remove the foil packets from the fire. Toast four thick slices of Beer and Cheese Bread on a grill over the fire until golden brown.

Unfold the foil and place the burgers on the toasted Beer and Cheese Bread. Spoon out any remaining mushrooms from the foil and place on top of the burgers. Serve immediately with Pan-fried New Potatoes.

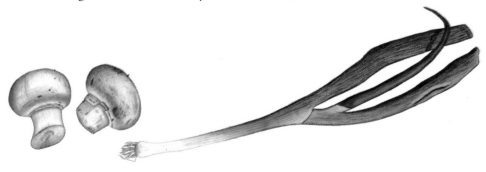

Beer and Cheese Bread

Makes 1 loaf (eight 2.5 cm/1 in slices)

135 g/4½ oz unsalted butter
350 g/12 oz plain flour
125 g/4 oz mature Cheddar cheese, grated
50 g/2 oz yellow cornmeal
4 teaspoons baking powder
1½ teaspoons salt
1 tablespoon honey
350 ml/12 fl oz beer
2 eggs, size 3, lightly beaten

Preheat the oven to 190°C/375°F/Gas 5.

Coat the inside of a 22.5 × 12.5 cm/9 × 5 in loaf tin with 15 g/½ oz of the butter.

In a large stainless steel bowl, thoroughly combine the flour, Cheddar, cornmeal, baking powder and salt.

Heat the remaining butter with the honey in a small saucepan over a medium heat. When the butter has melted, add to the dry ingredients. Add the beer and eggs. Stir well to combine.

Pour the mixture into the buttered loaf tin and bake for 45 minutes. Remove the bread from the oven and cool for 15 minutes before removing from the tin. Cool for at least 30 minutes before slicing.

Pan-fried New Potatoes

Serves 4

1 tablespoon salt
900 g/2 lb new potatoes, scrubbed but not peeled
4 slices smoked bacon, cut into 1 cm/½ in pieces
Salt and freshly ground black pepper
175 g/6 oz onions, sliced

Bring a large saucepan of water and 1 tablespoon salt to the boil. Add the potatoes, reduce the heat to medium-high and simmer for 20 minutes until potatoes are tender. Drain the potatoes and cool, uncovered, in the refrigerator.

Slice the cooled potatoes 1 cm/½ in. Heat a large non-stick frying pan over a medium-high heat. When the pan is hot, add the bacon and fry for 3½-4 minutes until lightly browned. Push the bacon to the edges of the pan and spread the potatoes on to the base of the pan. Season with salt and pepper, then cook undisturbed about 15 minutes until browned.

Spread the onions over the potatoes. Lightly season with salt and pepper and combine the onions, potatoes and bacon. Cook for an additional 10-15 minutes, stirring every 3-4 minutes. Remove from the heat and serve immediately.

The Pan-fried New Potatoes may be kept warm in a 90°C/200°F/Gas Low oven for up to 30 minutes before serving.

Westmoreland Bistro Burger
with Potato Salad

Makes 4 burgers

John and Caprial Pence
Chefs/Owners
Westmoreland Bistro and Wines
Portland, Oregon

THE RELATIONSHIP BETWEEN JOHN AND
CAPRIAL PENCE, BOTH GRADUATES OF THE
CULINARY INSTITUTE OF AMERICA, CAN
BE DESCRIBED AS NOTHING LESS THAN
REMARKABLE. AFTER MOVING TO SEATTLE
IMMEDIATELY FOLLOWING GRADUATION,
THIS HUSBAND-AND-WIFE TEAM WORKED
AT FULLERS RESTAURANT. JOHN
EVENTUALLY LEFT TO BECOME THE CHEF
AT LA FLEUR AND THEN AT PLACE PIGALLE.

AFTER CAPRIAL GAVE BIRTH TO THEIR
SON, JOHN STAYED HOME AND DEVOTED
HIS TIME AND ENERGY TO RAISING THE
CHILD. MEANWHILE, CAPRIAL BECAME
THE CHEF AT FULLERS, GAINING MUCH
NATIONAL AND INTERNATIONAL PRESS.
EVENTUALLY, JOHN RETURNED TO FULLERS
AS CO-CHEF WITH CAPRIAL.

IN 1992, THEIR LONG-HELD DREAM CAME
TRUE: THEY PURCHASED WESTMORELAND
BISTRO AND WINES, A TWENTY-THREE-SEAT
RESTAURANT AND RETAIL WINE STORE IN
PORTLAND, OREGON.

JOHN AND CAPRIAL HOPE YOU WILL
VISIT WHEN IN PORTLAND AND SAVOUR
A WESTMORELAND BISTRO BURGER
AT THE SOURCE.

6 medium spring onions,
  peeled
4 cloves garlic, peeled
2 tablespoons extra-virgin
  olive oil
1 tablespoon balsamic
  vinegar
1 teaspoon salt
½ teaspoon green
  peppercorns

½ teaspoon chopped fresh
  tarragon
750 g/1½ lb minced beef
1 45 cm/18 in loaf French
  bread, cut in half
  lengthways
4 thin slices cooked pancetta
  (see Note)
50 g/2 oz fresh goat's cheese,
  divided into 4 equal parts

Preheat the oven to 180°C/350°F/Gas 4.

Place the spring onions and garlic in a pie tin. Sprinkle with the olive oil
and balsamic vinegar and season with the salt, peppercorns and tarragon.
Cover the pie tin with aluminium foil. Place in the oven and roast the spring
onions and garlic about 35 minutes until tender.

Place the roasted spring onion-garlic mixture in the bowl of a food processor fitted with a metal blade and pulse until roughly puréed, about 10 seconds.
Transfer to a plate and place, uncovered, in the refrigerator to cool.

In a large stainless steel bowl, gently but thoroughly combine the minced
beef with the cooled spring onion-garlic mixture.

Gently form the minced beef mixture into four 175 g/6 oz oval-shaped
burgers, each 3 cm/1¼ in thick. Cover the burgers with cling film and refrigerate until needed.

Grill the burgers over a medium wood or charcoal fire. Cook as desired:
about 3-4 minutes on each side for rare, 6-7 minutes on each side for medium
and 8-9 minutes on each side for well done. (This burger may also be cooked
on a well-seasoned flat griddle or in a large non-stick frying pan over a

medium-high heat. Cook for about the same amout of time as listed for grilling.)

While the burgers are cooking, toast the French bread on the grill or griddle or in a non-stick frying pan, cut sides down, until golden brown. Cut the French bread halves into 10 cm/4 in long portions. Warm the cooked pancetta slices over the fire or in a non-stick frying pan for a few moments. Place each cooked burger on a bottom portion of the grilled bread and top each with a portion of the goat's cheese, 1 slice of the pancetta and the top portion of the grilled French bread. Serve immediately, accompanied by Potato Salad.

Note: Pancetta is an Italian bacon that is rolled into a solid round; it resembles belly of pork more than bacon. Look for pancetta at your local delicatessen or supermarket.

Potato Salad

Serves 4

 2 spring onions, trimmed and cut in half
   lengthways
50 ml/2 fl oz extra-virgin olive oil, plus
   1 tablespoon
900 g/2 lb small (about 6 cm/2½ in in diameter)
   unpeeled potatoes, such as Maris Peer
   Juice of 1 lemon
 1 tablespoon cider vinegar
 1 teaspoon chopped fresh thyme
 1 teaspoon salt
 ½ teaspoon cracked black pepper

Preheat the oven to 160°C/325°F/Gas 3.

Place the spring onions, cut sides down, in the bottom of a glass ovenproof dish or pie tin and drizzle them with 1 tablespoon olive oil. Cover the spring onions with aluminium foil and roast in the oven about 25 minutes until tender and golden brown. Remove the spring onions from the oven and allow them to cool, uncovered, in the olive oil at room temperature.

Place the potatoes in a large saucepan and cover with cold water. Bring to the boil over a high heat, then adjust the heat and simmer slowly for 35-40 minutes until potatoes are cooked through. Drain the water from the potatoes, then transfer to a large plate and cool, uncovered, in the refrigerator for at least 1 hour.

In a large stainless steel bowl, whisk together the remaining olive oil, lemon juice, cider vinegar, thyme, salt and pepper. Combine thoroughly.

Peel the skins from the cooled spring onions and thinly slice them lengthways.

Cut the cooled potatoes into quarters lengthways, then cut the quarters into slices.

Gently but thoroughly combine the roasted spring onions and sliced potatoes with the dressing. Serve immediately or store tightly covered in a non-metallic container for up to 3 days.

Vietnamese Sirloin Burger
with Cucumber and Carrot Salad

Makes 6 burgers

Nicole Routhier
Cookery Book Author
New York, New York

IF WRITING AN AWARD-WINNING COOKERY BOOK WAS NOT FOREMOST ON NICOLE ROUTHIER'S MIND WHEN SHE WAS A STUDENT AT THE CULINARY INSTITUTE OF AMERICA, IT IS NOW CERTAINLY AT THE TOP OF HER LIST OF ACHIEVEMENTS. NICOLE IS THE AUTHOR OF THE CRITICALLY ACCLAIMED *FOODS OF VIETNAM*. HER MOST RECENT BOOK, *COOKING UNDER WRAPS*, IS SURE TO PUT HER IN THE BIG LEAGUE OF BEST-SELLING AUTHORS.

NICOLE'S VIETNAMESE SIRLOIN BURGER IS A NATURAL OUTCOME OF HER BIRTHPLACE, TASTES AND INTERESTS. HAMBURGERS ARE ONE OF HER FAVOURITE FOODS AND SHE CONSIDERS THEM ONE OF THE MOST FLAVOURFUL AND SATISFYING MEALS. HER RECIPE IS AN ADAPTATION OF A POPULAR VIETNAMESE SPECIALITY.

This burger darkens very quickly if cooked over a fire that is too hot. The sugar in the fish sauce mixture makes the meat caramelise rapidly over a hot fire, so keep an eye on the flame. It is better to err in favour of a fire that is too low, which will increase cooking times, rather than a hot fire, which will render the burgers inedible.

65 g/2½ oz sugar
2 tablespoons fish sauce (see Note on following page)
2 tablespoons light soy sauce
2 tablespoons warm water
150 g/5 oz onions, finely chopped
4 teaspoons finely chopped garlic
¼ teaspoon freshly ground black pepper
900 g/2 lb minced sirloin
6 Onion Rolls (see page 89), cut in half
4 iceberg lettuce leaves, washed and dried
4 slices ripe red tomatoes

Heat the sugar in a medium non-stick frying pan over a medium-high heat, swirling the pan for about 2½ minutes until the sugar has thoroughly melted and is lightly browned. Remove from the heat and stir in the fish sauce, soy sauce and warm water, being careful to avoid splattering. Return the pan to a medium heat and stir the mixture constantly for 3-4 minutes until completely liquefied. Add the onions, garlic and pepper, stirring to combine. Transfer the mixture to a large stainless steel bowl and cool in the refrigerator until ready to use.

Gently but thoroughly combine the minced beef with the cooled fish sauce mixture. Cover with cling film and allow to stand at room temperature for 15 minutes (so the flavours blend).

Gently form the minced beef mixture into six 175 g/6 oz burgers, 2.5 cm/1 in thick. Cover with cling film and refrigerate until needed.

Grill the burgers over a low wood or charcoal fire. Cook as desired: 3-4 minutes on each side for rare, 5-6 minutes on each side for medium and 8-9 minutes on each side for well done. (This burger may also be cooked on a well-seasoned flat griddle or in a large non-stick frying pan over a medium heat. Cook for about the same amount of time as listed for grilling.)

Toast the rolls, cut sides down, on the grill or griddle or in a non-stick frying pan until golden brown. Place each burger on the bottom half of a roll, and top with 1 of the lettuce leaves, 1 of the tomato slices and the other half of the roll. Serve immediately accompanied by Cucumber and Carrot Salad.

Nicole says that in Vietnam, savoury-sweet burgers shaped into tiny patties are served accompanied by fresh lettuce leaves, soft noodles, pickles and lots of fresh herbs. In her recipe, Nicole has transformed the patties into a single burger and served them with Cucumber and Carrot Salad on the side.

Note: Not for the faint of nose, fish sauces pack an astonishingly odouriferous wallop. This limpid sauce takes some getting used to, but it will almost certainly lend a heady and pleasant flavour when used judiciously.

Cucumber and Carrot Salad

Serves 6

125 ml/4 fl oz unseasoned rice vinegar or distilled
    white vinegar
2 tablespoons sugar
½ teaspoon salt
125 ml/4 fl oz cold water
1 tablespoon fish sauce
½ teaspoon dried red chilli flakes
2 cucumbers, peeled, cut in half, seeded and
    thinly sliced diagonally
2 carrots, peeled and thinly sliced diagonally
1 small red onion, thinly sliced and rinsed well
    in cold water
2 tablespoons chopped fresh coriander

Heat the rice vinegar or white vinegar, sugar and salt in a saucepan over a medium-high heat. Bring to the boil and stir to dissolve the sugar. Transfer the mixture to a large stainless steel bowl. Stir in the cold water, fish sauce and red chilli flakes. Stir to combine. Allow the mixture to cool to room temperature. Add the vegetables and coriander, then gently toss to combine. Refrigerate and allow the mixture to marinate for at least 30 minutes before serving.

This salad will keep covered in the refrigerator for 2 or 3 days. Drain any excess liquid before serving.

Classic Grilled Hamburger
with Summer Vegetable Salad

Makes 4 burgers

L. Timothy Ryan
Vice President of Education
The Culinary Institute of America
Hyde Park, New York

AFTER FIVE YEARS OF INDUSTRY EXPERIENCE FOLLOWING HIS GRADUATION FROM THE INSTITUTE, TIM RETURNED TO HYDE PARK IN 1982 AS A MEMBER OF THE PROJECT TEAM THAT DEVELOPED THE AMERICAN BOUNTY RESTAURANT. DURING HIS TIME AS CHEF-INSTRUCTOR AT THE AMERICAN BOUNTY, TIM WAS SELECTED FOR THE 1983 *FOOD & WINE* MAGAZINE HONOUR ROLL OF AMERICAN CHEFS. SINCE THEN, TIM, NOW RESPONSIBLE FOR DIRECTING AND CO-ORDINATING THE INSTITUTE'S EDUCATIONAL PROGRAMMES, HAS SEEMINGLY WON ENOUGH GOLD IN NATIONAL AND INTERNATIONAL CULINARY COMPETITION TO SOLVE THE NATIONAL DEFICIT CRISIS.

TIM RYAN HAS THE DISTINCTION OF BEING THE YOUNGEST CHEF IN THE UNITED STATES TO RECEIVE MASTER CHEF CERTIFICATION FROM THE AMERICAN CULINARY FEDERATION. IN 1985, HE WAS NAMED A RECIPIENT OF THE MEDAL OF CULINARY EXCELLENCE FROM THE FRENCH REPUBLIC, CONSIDERED THE HIGHEST RECOGNITION OF CULINARY ACHIEVEMENT.

IT IS NO SURPRISE THAT AN AMERICAN OF SUCH IMPECCABLE CULINARY CREDENTIALS OFFERS THE QUINTESSENTIAL BURGER RECIPE.

900 g/2 lb minced beef
2 tablespoons cold water
Salt and freshly ground black pepper
4 Best Burger Buns (see page 109) or other favourite buns, cut in half

4 Iceberg lettuce leaves, washed and dried
4 slices ripe red tomatoes
Ketchup

In a large stainless steel bowl, gently but thoroughly combine the minced beef and cold water.

Gently form the beef into four 225 g/8 oz burgers, each 3 cm/1¼ in thick. Cover the burgers with cling film and refrigerate until needed.

Prior to grilling, generously season the burgers with salt and pepper.

Grill the burgers over a medium wood or charcoal fire. Cook as desired: 4-5 minutes on each side for rare, 6-7 minutes on each side for medium and 8-9 minutes on each side for well done. (This burger may also be cooked on a well-seasoned flat griddle or in a large non-stick frying pan over a medium-high heat. Cook for about the same amount of time as listed for grilling.)

Remove the burgers from the grill. Toast the buns, cut sides down, on the grill or griddle or in a non-stick fring pan until golden brown.

Serve the burgers on the toasted buns with the lettuce, tomatoes and ketchup and accompanied by Summer Vegetable Salad.

> *Tim suggests that you serve his Classic Grilled Hamburger with two other natural accompaniments: french fries, of course, and a very cold, strikingly refreshing glass of Coke.*

Summer Vegetable Salad

Serves 4

175 ml/6 fl oz extra-virgin olive oil
2 tablespoons balsamic vinegar
  Salt and pepper
2 cloves garlic, peeled
125 ml/4 fl oz fresh lemon juice
2 large artichokes
225 g/8 oz haricots vert, trimmed
4 plum tomatoes, peeled, seeded and chopped
1 large red pepper, roasted, skinned, seeded and cut into long thin strips
1 small red onion, thinly sliced
1/2 head frisée lettuce, cut into 5 cm/2 in pieces, washed and dried (see Note)
125 g/4 oz fresh mozzarella cheese, diced
1/2 bunch flat-leaf parsley, washed and dried
3 large basil leaves, washed, dried and cut into thin strips
1 bunch chives, thinly sliced

In a stainless steel bowl, whisk together the olive oil and balsamic vinegar. Adjust the seasoning with salt and pepper and combine thoroughly. Add the garlic and allow to marinate at room temperature for at least 30 minutes. Discard the garlic cloves before dressing the salad.

Bring a large saucepan of lightly salted water to the boil with 50 ml/2 fl oz of the lemon juice (this will be the cooking water). While the water is heating, remove the outer leaves from the artichokes. Slice off the flower about one-third of the way down from the top. Using a sharp-edged spoon, scrape out the hairy choke from the centre of the cut artichokes. Trim each stalk to about 0.5 cm/1/4 in. Place the artichokes, as soon as both have been cut and trimmed, into water acidulated with the remaining lemon juice. Keep the artichokes in this acidulated water until the cooking water begins to boil (do not keep the artichokes in the acidulated water for a prolonged period of time, or they will acquire a sour taste). Cook the artichokes in the boiling water for about 12 minutes until cooked through. Drain the cooked artichokes, then plunge them into ice water. When cool, peel the fibrous outer layer from the artichokes and slice lengthways.

Cook the green beans in lightly salted boiling water for 4-5 minutes until tender. Drain the beans, then immediately plunge them into ice water to stop the cooking and keep the beans bright green. Remove from the ice water and drain well.

In a large stainless steel bowl, combine the cooked artichokes, green beans, plum tomatoes, red pepper, red onions, frisée, mozzarella, parsley and basil. Toss together with the dressing, sprinkle the chives on top of the salad and serve immediately.

Note: Frisée is a delicate green with curly, frilly-edged leaves. You may substitute other endives such as the more commonly available curly endive.

> *To make the salad in advance (from a few hours to a day), prepare as described above, but do not toss the ingredients with the dressing until a few minutes before serving (otherwise, the green beans will discolour).*

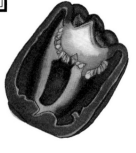

California Burger
with Best Parmesan Burger Buns

Makes 4 burgers

Charles Saunders

Executive Chef/Owner
East Side Oyster Bar & Grill
Sonoma, California

WHEN CHARLES SAUNDERS STUDIED POLITICAL SCIENCE AT AMERICAN UNIVERSITY IN WASHINGTON, D.C., HE FOCUSED ON INTERNATIONAL STUDIES AND FOREIGN LANGUAGES. BUT HIS SPARE TIME WAS FILLED WITH MANY HOURS OF GASTRONOMIC PEREGRINATIONS. SO IT IS NOT SURPRISING THAT SEVERAL YEARS LATER, CHARLES' EAGERNESS TO EXPAND HIS CULINARY INTERESTS BROUGHT HIM TO THE CULINARY INSTITUTE. FOLLOWING HIS GRADUATION, CHARLES' TWO WORLDS MERGED WHEN HE SERVED AS CHEF AT THE U.S. EMBASSY IN BERN, SWITZERLAND, FROM 1981 TO 1983, BECOMING THE FIRST AMERICAN CHEF AT AN AMERICAN EMBASSY IN EUROPE TO COOK AT THE PRIVATE RESIDENCE OF AN AMBASSADOR.

NOW ENSCONCED AT HIS OWN RESTAURANT, CHARLES HAS CONCENTRATED ON THE CUISINE OF CALIFORNIA FOR HIS BURGER RECIPE.

To add a spicy twist to the California Burgers, season the mayonnaise with some lemon juice, salt, freshly ground pepper and a pinch each of cayenne pepper, chilli powder and cumin.

---

350 g/12 oz lean minced beef
350 g/12 oz lean minced sirloin
  Salt and freshly ground
  black pepper
2 ripe avocados

4 red onion slices
4 Iceberg lettuce leaves,
  washed and dried
4 thick slices ripe tomatoes
4 tablespoons mayonnaise

In a large stainless steel bowl, gently combine the minced beef and minced sirloin.

Gently form the beef into four 175 g/6 oz burgers, each 2.5 cm/1 in thick. Season each with salt and pepper. Cover the burgers with cling film and refrigerate until needed.

Cut, stone and peel the avocados. Thinly slice the avocado halves from end to end. (The preparation of the avocados should be done just a few minutes before grilling the burgers; otherwise, the avocados will oxidize and discolour.)

Grill the burgers over a medium wood or charcoal fire. Cook as desired: 3-4 minutes on each side for rare, 5-6 minutes on each side for medium and 8-9 minutes on each side for well done. (This burger may also be cooked on a well-seasoned flat griddle or in a large non-stick frying pan over a medium-high heat. Cook for about the same amount of time as listed for grilling.)

While the burgers are being grilled, also grill the red onions. Place the onion slices on a well-oiled area of the grill and season with salt and pepper. Cook for 3-4 minutes on each side. (The onions could also be cooked in a non-stick frying pan.)

Remove the burgers and the onion slices from the grill. Cut 4 Best Parmesan Burger Buns in half. Toast the buns, cut sides down, on the grill or griddle or in a non-stick frying pan until golden brown. Spread 1/2 tablespoon mayonnaise on to each bun half. Place each burger on the bottom half of a bun and top with 1 of the lettuce leaves, 1 of the tomato slices, avocado slices, 1 of the grilled onion slices and a top bun half. Serve the burgers immediately.

The Best Burger Buns and The Best Parmesan Burger Buns

Makes 12 buns

½ teaspoon sugar
125 ml/4 fl oz warm water, plus 2 tablespoons
1 teaspoon dried yeast
475 g/17 oz plain flour
125 ml/4 fl oz milk
1 egg, size 3, at room temperature
2 tablespoons olive oil, plus 1 teaspoon
1 teaspoon salt
25 g/1 oz yellow cornmeal
1 egg white, size 3

125 g/4 oz Parmesan cheese, freshly grated
(for the Parmesan Burger Buns)

In the bowl of an electric mixer, dissolve the sugar in the warm water. Add the yeast and stir gently to dissolve. Allow the mixture to stand and foam for 6-8 minutes.

Place the mixing bowl on an electric mixer fitted with a dough hook. On top of the yeast mixture, add 450 g/1 lb flour (also add the Parmesan if making The Best Parmesan Burger Buns) and the milk, egg, 2 tablespoons olive oil and salt. Mix on a low speed for 1 minute, then scrape down the sides of the bowl. Continue to mix on low for 4-5 minutes until the dough forms a ball. If the dough attaches itself to the dough hook at any time, stop the mixer and pull the dough off the hook. (If a table-model electric mixer is not available, follow the directions using a hand-held mixer or kneading by hand. The mixing times will increase depending upon which alternative method is used.)

Knead the dough for 5-6 minutes on a clean, lightly floured work surface, using the remaining flour as necessary.

Coat the inside of a stainless steel bowl with the remaining 1 teaspoon olive oil. Place the dough in the bowl and wipe the bowl with the dough. Cover the bowl with a damp towel. Allow the dough to rise in a warm location for about 2 hours until the dough has doubled in volume.

Preheat the oven to 220°C/425°F/Gas 7.

Place the dough on a lightly floured work surface. Knock back the dough. Use a sharp knife to cut the dough into 12 equal portions. Shape each dough portion into a ball. Flatten each dough ball to 1 cm/½ in thick. Place the flattened dough balls on a baking tray that has been sprinkled with the cornmeal. Cover the dough with a damp towel and allow to rise in a warm location for about 45 minutes until doubled in size.

Whisk the egg white, then lightly brush over the flattened dough balls. Use a sharp knife or a razor blade to cut an X into the top of each dough ball, then bake for 12-14 minutes.

Allow the buns to cool thoroughly before slicing them horizontally.

The thoroughly cooled buns may be frozen for several weeks in polythene bags. Thaw the buns before grilling or toasting in the oven.

> *In the vernacular of the "Left Coast" (Charles' sobriquet for the American West Coast), this bun is indeed quite awesome, especially if prepared with the Parmesan cheese.*

West Indies Burger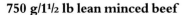
with Mango Chutney and Fried Plantains

Makes 4 burgers

Chris Schlesinger
Chef/Owner
East Coast Grill
Cambridge, Massachusetts

ANYONE WHO HAS EATEN CHRIS SCHLESINGER'S EXCITING FOOD WILL NOT NEED TO PONDER THE ORIGINS OF HIS WEST INDIES BURGER. MANY OF CHRIS' CULINARY INSPIRATIONS DERIVE FROM THE TIME HE "LABOURED" OVER HOT STOVES IN THE CARIBBEAN FOLLOWING HIS GRADUATION FROM THE CULINARY INSTITUTE OF AMERICA.

SINCE OPENING THE EAST COAST GRILL IN 1985, CHRIS HAS FIRED THE CULINARY LANDSCAPE WITH HIS EXPLOSIVE FLAVOURS. HIS BEST-SELLING COOKBOOK *THE THRILL OF THE GRILL* IS A TRIBUTE TO HIS INCENDIARY CUISINE.

> *Chris insists that the only beverage allowable with his burger is a very cold can of beer.*

750 g/1½ lb lean minced beef
3 tablespoons chopped fresh coriander
1 tablespoon finely chopped garlic
2 teaspoons fresh lime juice
1 teaspoon curry powder
1 teaspoon ground cumin
1 teaspoon ground allspice
3 – 5 dashes Tabasco Sauce
Salt and freshly cracked black pepper
4 Best Burger Buns (see page 109), cut in half, or other favourite bread

In a large stainless steel bowl, gently but thoroughly combine the minced beef with the coriander, garlic, lime juice, curry powder, cumin, allspice, Tabasco Sauce and salt and pepper to taste.

Gently form the seasoned beef into four 175 g/6 oz burgers, each 2 cm/¾ in thick. Cover the burgers with cling film and refrigerate until needed.

Grill the burgers over a medium wood or charcoal fire. Cook as desired: 3-4 minutes on each side for rare, 5-6 minutes on each side for medium and 8-9 minutes on each side for well done. (This burger may also be cooked on a well-seasoned flat griddle or in a non-stick frying pan over a medium-high heat. Cook for about the same amount of time as listed for grilling.)

Remove the burgers from the grill. Toast the buns, cut sides down, on the grill or griddle or in a non-stick frying pan until golden brown. Place each burger on the bottom half of a bun and top with Mango Chutney. Cover the chutney with the top half of the bun and serve with Fried Plantains.

Mango Chutney

Makes about 900 g/2 lb

2 tablespoons vegetable oil
2 large onions, diced
3 ripe mangoes, peeled, stoned and cut into
    large chunks
4 tablespoons tightly packed light brown sugar
4 tablespoons sugar
40 g/1½ oz raisins
1 tablespoon molasses
1 teaspoon salt
½ teaspoon freshly cracked white pepper
¼ teaspoon ground allspice
125 ml/4 fl oz white vinegar
2 tablespoons fresh lemon juice

Heat the vegetable oil in a large stainless steel saucepan over a medium heat. When hot, add the onions. Cook for 6-8 minutes until the onions are translucent.

Add the mango chunks, stir and cook for 4 minutes.

Add the remaining ingredients except half the white vinegar and the lemon juice. Reduce the heat to low and simmer, uncovered, for 1 hour, stirring frequently to prevent the mixture from burning. (If necessary, add 1-2 tablespoons water during the simmering to prevent the sticking and burning of the mixture.)

Remove the mixture from the heat. Add the remaining white vinegar and the lemon juice, and combine thoroughly. Cool the chutney in an ice-water bath until cold. Refrigerate the chutney in a stainless steel or other non-corrosive container. Keep refrigerated for 12 hours before serving. The chutney will keep tightly covered in the refrigerator for up to 6 weeks.

Chris Schlesinger recommends that the chutney be served at room temperature to optimise its flavour.

Fried Plantains

Serves 4

2 green plantains (see Note)
Vegetable oil for deep-frying
Salt and freshly cracked black pepper

Peel the plantains. Cut each plantain into 4 pieces, each about 5 cm/2 in long.

Heat the vegetable oil in a deep-fat fryer (or high-sided, heavy-based saucepan) to a temperature of 180°C/350°F.

Drop the plantain pieces into the hot oil, 2 at a time, and cook them for 2-3 minutes until well browned. Remove them from the oil and drain on kitchen towels.

Stand each fried section upright on a table. Using a heavy frying pan, mash each round as flat as a pancake using steady pressure rather than sharp blows.

Put the mashed sections back into the hot oil, 2 at a time and cook for 2 minutes or until the entire surface is golden brown.

Remove, drain and season the fried plantains liberally with salt and pepper.

Note: Sometimes known as the cooking banana, the plantain has become very popular, creating great demand at most well-stocked produce markets.

Although the hard and starchy texture of a green plantain yields the most favourable results for this recipe, it is also feasible to use riper plantains. The peel of a more mature plantain will range from brown to black. Do not be put off by a lack of aesthetics; riper plantains yield a creamy and sweet fruit.

These fried plantains were fondly nicknamed "tropical french fries" in The Thrill of the Grill.

Prawn Boulette Po' Boy Burger
with Home-made Worcestershire Sauce
and Creole Sauce

Makes 4 burgers

Jamie Shannon
Executive Chef
Commander's Palace
New Orleans, Louisiana

JAMIE SHANNON'S CULINARY EXPERIENCE
BEGAN DURING HIS BOYHOOD ON
THE NEW JERSEY SHORE. HE SPENT
MANY SUMMER DAYS THERE AT HIS
GRANDPARENTS' FARM, FEASTING ON
GREAT HOME-MADE DISHES PREPARED
FROM INGREDIENTS FRESH FROM THE
LAND. FOODS THAT DID NOT COME
FROM THE FARM CAME FROM SICILIAN
FISHERMEN, FROM CRAB TRAPS JAMIE SET
IN THE "BACKYARD", AND FROM STREET
VENDORS, WHO SOLD PASTA AND CHEESES.

AFTER LEARNING THE BASIC COOKING
TECHNIQUES WHILE WORKING IN A LOCAL
CAFETERIA, JAMIE POLISHED HIS SKILLS IN
RESTAURANTS IN THE RESORT TOWN OF
WILDWOOD, NEW JERSEY, AND THEN
ENROLLED AT THE CULINARY INSTITUTE OF
AMERICA. THERE HE DECIDED TO PURSUE
REGIONAL AMERICAN COOKING AS HIS
SPECIALITY, AND FOLLOWING GRADUATION,
HE CHOSE NEW ORLEANS AS HIS HOME
BASE. JAMIE JOINED COMMANDER'S PALACE
IN 1984 AS A SAUCIER, WORKED HIS WAY
THROUGH THE KITCHEN BRIGADE, AND
EVENTUALLY BECAME EXECUTIVE CHEF
OF THIS INTERNATIONALLY ACCLAIMED
RESTAURANT.

*Enjoy this zesty burger with a cold
beer or experiment with a vivaciously
fruity and spicy Gewürztraminer.*

1 teaspoon groundnut oil
65 g/2½ oz onions, finely chopped
2 teaspoons finely chopped garlic
65 g/2½ oz celery, finely diced
40 g/1½ oz red pepper, finely diced
40 g/1½ oz green pepper, finely diced
40 g/1½ oz yellow pepper, finely diced
1 small, hot red or green chilli, roasted, skinned seeded and very finely chopped

750 g/1½ lb medium prawns, peeled and deveined
2 tablespoons chopped fresh chives
2 tablespoons chopped fresh parsley
1 tablespoon chopped fresh basil
1 tablespoon chopped fresh thyme
Salt and white pepper
1 loaf French bread

Heat the groundnut oil in a large non-stick frying pan over a medium-high heat. When hot, add the onions and garlic and cook until the onions are translucent. Add the celery, peppers and no more than 1 teaspoon finely chopped chilli and continue to cook for 5 minutes. Transfer the mixture to a plate and place, uncovered, in the refrigerator to cool.

Mince the prawns through a meat mincer fitted with a coarse mincing plate into a large stainless steel bowl. Gently but thoroughly combine the minced prawns with the cooled vegetable mixture, chives, parsley, basil and thyme. Season with salt and pepper.

Gently form the mixture into eight 100 g/3½ oz burgers, each 2 cm/¾ in thick. Cover the burgers with cling film and refrigerate until needed.

Preheat the oven to 110°C/225°F/Gas ¼.

Trim each end of the loaf of French bread. Cut the trimmed loaf into four 10 cm/4 in long portions. Cut each portion in half. Crisp the bread in the oven while cooking the burgers.

Grill the prawn burgers over a medium-high wood or charcoal fire, 5-6 minutes on each side, basting with about 1 teaspoon Home-made Worcestershire Sauce per burger. Serve 2 of the prawn burgers on each portion of the crusty French bread, topped with Creole Sauce.

Home-made Worcestershire Sauce

Makes about 350 ml/12 fl oz

2 teaspoons olive oil
175 g/6 oz onions, diced
3 tablespoons grated fresh horseradish
1 small, hot green or red chilli, seeded and chopped
1 tablespoon very finely chopped garlic
450 ml/¾ pint distilled white vinegar
350 g/12 oz dark corn syrup; see Note on page 38
175 g/6 oz molasses
125 ml/4 fl oz water
1 lemon, peeled and chopped
1 anchovy fillet
6 whole cloves
2 teaspoons salt
½ teaspoon cracked black pepper

Heat the olive oil in a large saucepan over a medium-high heat. When hot, add the onions, horseradish, chilli and garlic and cook for 3-4 minutes, stirring frequently. Add the remaining ingredients and stir to combine. Bring the mixture to the boil. Reduce the heat and simmer for 2½-3 hours until slightly thickened.

Strain through a fine-mesh sieve or muslin, then cool in an ice-water bath and store, tightly covered, in the refrigerator.

Although Jamie stores his Home-made Worcestershire Sauce in wooden vats, the sauce can be kept tightly covered in a non-corrosive container in the refrigerator for up to several weeks.

This Home-made Worcestershire Sauce has as many uses as you might imagine. Since the yield for this recipe is more than will be necessary to baste 4 Prawn Boulette Po' Boy Burgers, you will probably find yourself basting chicken, chops and fish with this wonderful concoction.

Creole Sauce

Makes about 600 ml/1 pint

2 teaspoons extra-virgin olive oil
1 teaspoon paprika
1 small onion, peeled and thinly sliced
65 g/2½ oz celery, diced
40 g/1½ oz green pepper, diced
40 g/1½ oz red pepper, diced
40 g/1½ oz yellow pepper, diced
1 teaspoon very finely chopped garlic
1 small, hot red or green chilli, roasted, skinned, seeded and very finely chopped
2 teaspoons sugar
50 ml/2 fl oz chicken stock
50 ml/2 fl oz tomato juice
2 teaspoons balsamic vinegar
3 plum tomatoes, peeled, seeded and chopped
1 tablespoon chopped fresh parsley
1 teaspoon chopped fresh basil
1 teaspoon chopped fresh thyme
Salt

Heat the olive oil in a large saucepan over a medium heat. When hot, add the paprika and cook for 1 minute, stirring constantly to avoid scorching. Add the onion and cook for 2-3 minutes. Then add the celery, green, red and yellow peppers, garlic and chilli and continue to cook for an additional 3-4 minutes. Add the sugar and stir to dissolve. Add the chicken stock, tomato juice and balsamic vinegar and stir to combine. Add the plum tomatoes, parsley, basil and thyme and stir gently to combine. Allow the sauce to simmer for 4-5 minutes. Adjust the seasoning with salt. Serve immediately, or keep warm in a double boiler for up to 1 hour before using.

The sauce may be cooled in an ice-water bath, then covered and refrigerated for up to 3 days before using. Heat the sauce to a simmer before serving.

"Trini" Burger
with Tropical Fruit Salad

Makes 4 burgers

Arnym Solomon
Vice President of Chain Accounts
CPC Foodservice
Franklin Park, Illinois

SCION OF A PROMINENT TRINIDADIAN
FOOD-SERVICE FAMILY, ARNYM SOLOMON
CARRIES ON THE TRADITION HIS FATHER
SET FORTH FOR THE SOLOMON CLAN.
ARNYM'S DAD, CARL, IS WELL KNOWN
THROUGHOUT THE CARIBBEAN AS AN
EXECUTIVE CHEF, AS WELL AS ONE OF THE
FOUNDERS OF TRINIDAD'S IMPORTANT
CULINARY TRAINING FACILITY, THE JOHN
S. DONALDSON TECHNICAL INSTITUTE.
ARNYM HAS SERVED IN FOOD AND
BEVERAGE POSITIONS THROUGHOUT THE
WORLD, INCLUDING THE HUNTINGTON
HILTON IN DALLAS, THE WALDORF-ASTORIA
HOTEL IN NEW YORK CITY, THE TRINIDAD
HILTON IN PORT OF SPAIN, TRINIDAD, AND
HIS ALMA MATER, THE CULINARY
INSTITUTE OF AMERICA.

THE PLACE OF ORIGIN FOR STEEL BANDS
AND CALYPSO, TRINIDAD IS EXCITING,
VIBRANT AND COLOURFUL. LIKEWISE IS
ARNYM SOLOMON'S BURGER RECIPE.

900 g/2 lb lean minced beef
4 tablespoons Worcestershire sauce
1 tablespoon chopped fresh thyme
1 teaspoon ground cumin
1 teaspoon cayenne pepper
125 g/4 oz onions, finely chopped
25 g/1 oz Cheddar cheese, finely diced

Salt and white pepper
4 Best Burger Buns (see page 109), cut in half
4 tablespoons mayonnaise
4 large Iceberg lettuce leaves, washed and dried
8 thin slices ripe tomatoes
1/2 medium papaya, peeled, seeded and thinly sliced

In a large stainless steel bowl, gently but thoroughly combine the minced beef with the Worcestershire sauce, thyme, cumin and cayenne pepper.

Gently form the minced beef mixture into eight 125 g/4 oz patties, each 2 cm/3/4 in thick.

Use a metal spoon to make a small, shallow indentation in the centre of 4 of the beef patties. Combine the onions and Cheddar. Divide this mixture into 4 equal portions and place a portion in each indentation. Top with another patty and gently form into a burger, making sure to seal all open edges. Season the burgers with salt and white pepper. Cover the burgers with cling film and refrigerate until needed.

Grill the burgers over a medium wood or charcoal fire. Cook as desired: 5-6 minutes on each side for rare, 6-7 minutes on each side for medium and

9-10 minutes on each side for well done. (This burger may also be cooked on a well-seasoned flat griddle or in a large non-stick frying pan over a medium-high heat. Cook for about the same amount of time as listed for grilling.)

Remove the burgers from the grill. Toast the buns, cut sides down, on the grill or griddle or in a non-stick frying pan until golden brown.

Spread ½ tablespoon mayonnaise on to each burger bun half. Place 1 of the lettuce leaves on the bottom half of each bun, then top each with a burger, 2 of the tomato slices, 2 of the papaya slices and the top half of the bun. Serve immediately accompanied by Tropical Fruit Salad.

Tropical Fruit Salad

Serves 4

2 tablespoons coconut milk
2 tablespoons malt vinegar
1 tablespoon dark rum
1 tablespoon fresh lime juice
¼ teaspoon seeded and finely chopped
**   fresh small, hot red or green chilli**
3 tablespoons groundnut oil
1 ripe medium papaya, about 900 g/2 lb,
**   peeled, seeded and cut into large chunks**
1 ripe medium mango, stoned, peeled
**   and cut into large chunks**
1 ripe medium banana, peeled and sliced
1 kiwi fruit, peeled and sliced
75 g/3 oz cashews, toasted
2 tablespoons grated fresh coconut
½ teaspoon chopped fresh coriander

In a stainless steel bowl, whisk together the coconut milk, malt vinegar, rum, lime juice and chilli. Continue to whisk the mixture while pouring in a slow, steady stream of the groundnut oil. Add the papaya, mango, banana and kiwi fruit to the dressing and gently toss. Portion one-quarter of dressed fruits per serving and garnish with the cashews, coconut and coriander. Serve immediately.

The dressed tropical fruits may be stored, covered, in the refrigerator for 2 or 3 days. Keep the cashews, coconut and coriander separate and garnish just before serving.

This lively fruit salad is not only great with the "Trini" Burger, it is also delicious as a light first course or as a dessert served with a scoop or two of a tropical fruit sorbet and a splash of dark rum.

Jumbo Lump Crab Meat Burger

with Marinated Red Cabbage Coleslaw

Makes 4 burgers

Rodney Stoner

Director of Food and Beverage
The Greenbrier Hotel
White Sulphur Springs, West Virginia

FOOD SERVICE HAS BEEN ROD STONER'S LIFE FROM THE TIME OF HIS EARLY TEENS, WHEN HE WORKED FOR HIS GRANDFATHER IN THE FAMILY CATERING BUSINESS. AFTER GRADUATING FROM THE CULINARY INSTITUTE OF AMERICA IN 1965, ROD WORKED AT THE BOAR'S HEAD INN IN CHARLOTTESVILLE, VIRGINIA. HE THEN BECAME A CULINARY APPRENTICE AT THE GREENBRIER BEFORE JOINING THE COLONIAL WILLIAMSBURG FOUNDATION.

ROD RETURNED TO THE GREENBRIER, ONE OF ONLY A HANDFUL OF OPERATIONS IN THE UNITED STATES BEARING THE MOBIL FIVE-STAR AND THE AMERICAN AUTOMOBILE ASSOCIATION FIVE-DIAMOND AWARDS, IN 1977. IN ADDITION TO BEING DIRECTOR OF FOOD AND BEVERAGE FOR THE GREENBRIER, HE ACTS AS VICE PRESIDENT OF FOOD AND BEVERAGE FOR THE GREENBRIER RESORT MANAGEMENT COMPANY, WHICH OWNS AND OPERATES OTHER RESORT PROPERTIES.

SINCE THE GREENBRIER RESORT USES OVER 4,500 KILOGRAMS (10,000 POUNDS) OF CRAB MEAT PER YEAR, ROD THOUGHT A SPECIAL BURGER USING CRAB MEAT WAS A NATURAL. THIS JUMBO LUMP CRAB MEAT BURGER SHOULD MAKE A NOTEWORTHY ADDITION TO YOUR RECIPE FILE.

65 g/2½ oz unsalted butter
65 g/2½ oz celery, diced
4 tablespoons thinly sliced spring onions
Salt and pepper
3 tablespoons mayonnaise
2 tablespoons soured cream
1 teaspoon seasoned salt
1 teaspoon fresh lemon juice

450 g/1 lb fresh jumbo lump blue crab meat, well picked of shell (see Note)
4 sourdough English muffins, split
4 slices Muenster cheese
50 g/2 oz Asiago cheese, grated (see Note)

Heat 15 g/½ oz butter in a small non-stick frying pan over a medium-high heat. When melted, add the celery and cook for 2 minutes. Add the spring onions, lightly season with salt and pepper and cook for an additional minute. Transfer the celery and spring onions to a plate and place, uncovered, in the refrigerator to cool.

In a stainless steel bowl, whisk together the mayonnaise, soured cream, seasoned salt and lemon juice. Fold in the cooled celery and spring onions. Adjust the seasoning with salt and pepper and combine thoroughly. Very gently fold in the crab meat, being careful not to break up the pieces.

Gently form the crab meat mixture into four 150 g/5 oz burgers, each 2.5 cm/1 in thick. Cover the burgers with cling film and refrigerate until needed.

Preheat the grill.

Heat 15 g/½ oz butter in a large non-stick frying pan over a medium-high heat. When hot, pan-fry the crab burgers for 4 minutes on each side until golden brown.

While the crab burgers are frying, toast the English muffins under the grill or in a toaster. Spread the remaining butter on to the split sides of the toasted muffins.

Place the crab burgers on the buttered sides of 4 of the English muffin halves. Place a slice of the Muenster on top of each. Sprinkle each with one-quarter of the Asiago. Place on a baking tray and brown the cheese under the grill for 2–3 minutes. Top with the other muffin halves and serve immediately accompanied by Marinated Red Cabbage Coleslaw.

Note: "Jumbo lump" refers to the 2 large pieces of white meat from the body of a cooked crab. This is the most expensive part of the blue crab, but quite assuredly the best. Less expensive crab meat may be used for this recipe; however, it will not deliver the same texturally pleasing qualities of the jumbo lump.

Asiago is a semi-hard, mildly flavoured cheese produced both in Italy and in Wisconsin. Look for Asiago cheese in a speciality cheese shop. If Asiago is not available, substitute Romano or Parmesan cheese.

Marinated Red Cabbage Coleslaw

Serves 4

175 ml/6 fl oz sherry vinegar
125 ml/4 fl oz extra-virgin olive oil
2 tablespoons muscavado sugar
1 tablespoon dry mustard
1 teaspoon celery seeds
1 teaspoon salt
1 teaspoon ground white pepper
1 head red cabbage, cored and thinly sliced
1 onion, thinly sliced

Heat the sherry vinegar, olive oil, sugar, mustard, celery seeds, salt and pepper in a saucepan over a high heat. Bring to the boil. Place the cabbage and onion in a large stainless steel bowl. Pour the boiling dressing over the cabbage and onions (do not stir), cover with cling film and marinate in the refrigerator for 4–6 hours. Toss the cabbage and onions together and serve. The coleslaw may be stored, tightly covered, in a non-corrosive container for 2 or 3 days.

Duck Burger

with Wild Rice Buns, Caramelised Sliced Onions and Tarragon Mushrooms

Makes 4 burgers

Paul Sturkey
Chef/Owner
Pigall's Cafe
Cincinnati, Ohio

A NATIVE MID-WESTERNER, PAUL STURKEY GRADUATED FROM THE UNIVERSITY OF AKRON, IN AKRON, OHIO, BEFORE ATTENDING THE CULINARY INSTITUTE OF AMERICA.

CHEF STURKEY HAS COMPILED AN IMPRESSIVE LIST OF ACCOMPLISHMENTS SINCE HIS GRADUATION. FROM 1980 TO 1985 HE FOUNDED AND DEVELOPED THE GREATER CINCINNATI CULINARY ACADEMY, WHICH TRAINS COOKS WHO ASPIRE TO BECOME CHEFS. IN 1987, AS EXECUTIVE CHEF, HE OPENED THE RESTAURANT AT THE PHOENIX IN DOWNTOWN CINCINNATI, WHICH WAS CHOSEN THAT YEAR AS ONE OF THE TEN BEST NEW RESTAURANTS IN AMERICA BY *ESQUIRE* MAGAZINE. AND IN APRIL 1991, PAUL STURKEY REOPENED PIGALL'S, A HISTORIC LANDMARK RESTAURANT IN DOWNTOWN CINCINNATI THAT FOR OVER THIRTY YEARS HAD BEEN ONE OF THAT CITY'S TWO FIVE-STAR RESTAURANTS. RENAMED PIGALL'S CAFE, UNDER CHEF STURKEY'S MASTERFUL HAND, THE RESTAURANT HAS TAKEN CINCINNATI BY STORM, AND IN A VERY SHORT TIME IT HAS CREATED A NEW TRADITION IN CINCINNATI DINING.

125 ml/4 fl oz chicken stock or water
2 teaspoons finely chopped garlic
750 g/1½ lb boneless and skinless duck breast meat, trimmed of fat and cut into 2.5 cm/1 in pieces (or 750 g/ 1½ lb minced duck breast meat)

225 g/8 oz pork fat, diced
2 tablespoons chopped fresh sage
2 teaspoons chopped fresh tarragon
1 tablespoon salt
1 tablespoon freshly ground black pepper

Heat the chicken stock or water in a small saucepan over a medium-high heat. Bring to the simmer. Poach the garlic in the simmering stock for 3-5 minutes. Strain the garlic and discard the stock. Transfer the garlic onto a small plate and place, uncovered, in the refrigerator to cool.

If using duck meat pieces, mince them through a meat mincer fitted with a coarse mincing plate into a large stainless steel bowl.

Add the pork fat, chilled garlic, sage, tarragon, salt and pepper to the minced duck meat. Gently but thoroughly combine.

Gently form the minced duck mixture into four 225 g/8 oz burgers, each 3 cm/1¼ in thick. Cover the burgers with cling film and refrigerate until needed.

Grill the burgers over a medium charcoal or wood fire. Cook until about medium, 8-9 minutes on each side. (This burger may also be cooked on a well-seasoned flat griddle or in a large non-stick frying pan over a medium-high heat. Cook for about the same amount of time as listed for grilling.)

Remove the burgers from the grill. Cut 4 Wild Rice Buns in half. Toast the buns, cut sides down, on the grill or griddle or in a non-stick frying pan until golden brown.

Serve the Duck Burgers on the buns, topped with Caramelised Sliced Onions and Tarragon Mushrooms.

Wild Rice Buns

Makes 8 buns

900 ml/1½ pints water, plus 1 tablespoon
100 g/4 oz wild rice
1½ teaspoons salt
175 ml/6 fl oz milk
25 g/1 oz unsalted butter
2 tablespoons cottage cheese
2 tablespoons sugar
1 tablespoon dried yeast
500 g/18 oz plain flour
150 g/5 oz onions, finely diced
1 egg yolk, size 3

Bring the water to the boil in a small saucepan.

Add the wild rice and ½ teaspoon salt. Adjust the heat to allow the rice to simmer for about 1½ hours until each wild rice grain is completely open. Remove from the heat and drain in a colander. Allow the rice to cool to room temperature for 10-15 minutes.

Heat the milk, butter, cottage cheese, sugar and remaining 1 teaspoon salt in a saucepan over a medium heat to a temperature of 50°C/120°F. Remove from the heat and pour into the bowl of an electric mixer. Add the yeast and stir gently to dissolve. Allow the mixture to stand and foam for 8 minutes.

Add 400 g/14 oz of the flour, the cooked wild rice and the onions. Combine on the low speed of an electric mixer fitted with a dough hook for 2 minutes. Scrape down the sides of the bowl, then continue to mix on a low speed for about 5 minutes until the dough is thoroughly combined and smooth. (If a table-model electric mixer is not available, use a hand-held mixer or knead by hand. The mixing times will increase depending upon which alternative method is used.)

Remove the bowl from the mixer and cover with a towel or cling film. Allow the dough to rise in a warm location for about 1 hour until it has doubled in volume.

Place the dough on a clean, lightly floured work surface, using the remaining flour as necessary. Use a sharp knife to cut the dough into 8 equal portions. Shape each portion into a round ball. Divide the dough balls on to 2 baking trays lined with baking parchment. Cover each baking tray with cling film and allow to rest for 10 minutes.

Preheat the oven to 180°C/350°F/Gas 4.

Slightly flatten each dough ball. Allow to rise in a warm location for 20-25 minutes until doubled in size.

Whisk the egg yolk and remaining 1 tablespoon water, then lightly brush the top of each flattened dough ball with this egg wash.

Bake for 20-25 minutes, rotating the baking trays from top to bottom and front to back about halfway through the baking time.

Allow the Wild Rice Buns to cool thoroughly before cutting in half.

The buns will keep fresh for 2 or 3 days stored in a sealed polythene bag at room temperature.

Wild rice, which is actually a grass and not a grain, lends a very specific flavour to this bun. The rice must be thoroughly cooked, that is, until each grain has completely opened—or it will harden as it is baked.

Caramelised Sliced Onions

Serves 4

2 onions, cut into eight 1 cm/¹/₂ in thick slices

Heat a large non-stick frying pan over a medium heat. When the pan is hot, place the onion slices in the pan and caramelise for 20 minutes on each side. The caramelised onions may be used immediately or kept warm in a 90°C/200°F/Gas Low oven for up to 30 minutes before serving.

Tarragon Mushrooms

Serves 4

50 g/2 oz unsalted butter
50 ml/2 fl oz dry white wine
1 tablespoon chopped fresh tarragon
300 g/10 oz fresh shiitake mushrooms, stalks removed and sliced

Heat the butter and white wine in a medium non-stick frying pan over a medium-high heat. When the butter has melted, add the tarragon and cook for about 6 to 8 seconds. Add the shiitake mushrooms and cook for 4-5 minutes. Serve immediately on the Duck Burgers.

The aroma that wafts from the Duck Burgers when they are grilling is sure to seduce the olfactory receptors. This is "outdoor" food at its best. Be prepared to part with this recipe as Paul Sturkey did, for once consumed, this Duck Burger will be forever remembers and craved.

Aztec Burger

with Chocolate Buns, Rubblechuck Fries and Raspberry Relish

Makes 4 burgers

John Twichell
Pastry Chef
The Trellis Restaurant
Williamsburg, Virginia

HOW DOES A PASTRY CHEF GET TANGLED UP IN A COOKERY BOOK ABOUT BURGERS? IT WAS NOT A MATTER OF BEING COERCED; RATHER, IT WAS A FEAR OF BEING LEFT OUT OF ALL THE FUN THAT PROMPTED JOHN TO CREATE THIS UNUSUAL BURGER.

JOHN TWICHELL HAS WORKED AT THE TRELLIS SINCE HE GRADUATED FROM THE CULINARY INSTITUTE OF AMERICA IN 1986. HE STARTED IN THE PANTRY, QUICKLY ADVANCING TO OTHER STATIONS. WITHIN A YEAR AND A HALF, HE WAS ASSISTANT PASTRY CHEF; HE BECAME PASTRY CHEF IN FEBRUARY 1988 AT THE AGE OF TWENTY-TWO.

ON A BUSY DAY, JOHN MASTERMINDS THE TRANSFORMATION OF EIGHTEEN TO TWENTY-TWO KILOGRAMS (FORTY TO FIFTY POUNDS) OF CHOCOLATE INTO DECADENT DESSERTS SERVED TO CHOCOLATE LOVERS. JOHN IS ALSO RESPONSIBLE FOR THE DAILY PRODUCTION OF A VARIETY OF BREADS AND THE RENOWNED TRELLIS BREAD STICKS.

ALTHOUGH JOHN HAS GONE OVER THE TOP IN DEVISING HIS AZTEC BURGER, SO NAMED BECAUSE THE AZTECS WERE KNOWN TO OFFER AN UNSWEETENED CHOCOLATE DRINK TO THEIR VICTIMS OF HUMAN SACRIFICE, THIS CUNNING CONFECTIONER KNOWS NO OTHER WAY.

175 ml/6 fl oz double cream
225 g/8 oz plain chocolate, broken into 15 g/^{1}/$_2$ oz pieces
50 g/2 oz white chocolate, broken into 15 g/^{1}/$_2$ oz pieces

8 thick slices peeled kiwi fruit
15 g/^{1}/$_2$ oz white chocolate, finely grated

Heat the cream in a saucepan over a medium-high heat. Bring to the boil. Place the plain chocolate pieces in a large stainless steel bowl. Pour the boiling cream over the chocolate and allow to stand for 5 minutes. Stir with a whisk until smooth. Scrape the sides of the bowl. Whisk again to ensure that there are no lumps. Pour the mixture on to a baking tray and refrigerate for 35 minutes until firm but not hard.

Draw 4 circles, approximately 9 cm/3^1/$_2$ in in diameter, on to a sheet of baking parchment (the pencil lines should be dark enough to show through the paper). Place the paper, pencilled side down, on to a clean baking tray. Use a rubber spatula to scrape the chilled chocolate from the baking tray into a piping bag fitted with a small star nozzle.

Fill the traced parchment circles with the chilled chocolate, starting in the centre and piping towards the outside of each circle to form 1 cm/^{1}/$_2$ in thick "burgers".

Place the baking tray of formed burgers in the freezer for about 30 minutes until very firm. Cover the burgers with cling film and refrigerate until needed.

Make the white chocolate "cheese slices" for the burgers. Heat 2.5 cm/1 in water in the bottom half of a double boiler over a low heat. Place the white chocolate pieces in the top half of the double boiler. Using a rubber spatula, constantly stir the white chocolate for 4 minutes until melted. Remove chocolate from heat and continue stirring for about 3 minutes until chocolate reaches a temperature of 30°C/85°F.

Cover the bottom of a baking tray with cling film, using your hands to smooth out the wrinkles. Pour the melted white chocolate on to the baking tray and spread it to a square measuring 18 × 18 cm/7 × 7 in. Refrigerate

about 3 minutes until firm but not hard. Cut the white chocolate into 4 equal squares. Refrigerate the squares about 10 minutes until completely hardened.

Remove the burgers from the baking parchment and place on the bottom halves of the Chocolate Buns. Place 1 slice of the white chocolate "cheese" on top of each burger, then place 2 of the kiwi fruit slices (for the pickles) on top of the white chocolate "cheese". Top with the top bun halves. Sprinkle the finely grated white chocolate (for the sesame seeds, of course) over the top of each bun and serve accompanied by Rubblechuck Fries and Raspberry Relish.

Chocolate Buns

Makes 4 buns

100 g/3½ oz plain flour, plus 1 tablespoon
3 tablespoons unsweetened cocoa
½ teaspoon baking soda
½ teaspoon salt
50 g/2 oz unsalted butter, softened, plus 10 g/⅓ oz
25 g/1 oz dark chocolate, chopped into 5 cm/¼ in pieces
100 g/3½ oz light brown sugar
1 egg, size 3
½ teaspoon vanilla essence
½ teaspoon red raspberry vinegar
125 ml/4 fl oz boiling water

Preheat the oven to 160°C/325°F/Gas 3.

Sift together 100 g/3½ oz flour and the cocoa, baking soda and salt on to greaseproof paper, then set aside until needed.

Lightly coat four 225 g/8 oz ovenproof ramekins with 2 teaspoons butter. Dust the insides with the remaining 1 tablespoon flour. Shake out any excess flour.

Heat 2.5 cm/1 in water in the bottom half of a double boiler over a medium heat. Place the dark chocolate in the top half of the double boiler. Tightly cover the top with cling film. Allow to heat for 2-3 minutes. Remove from the heat and stir until smooth. Set aside until needed.

Place the brown sugar and remaining 50 g/2 oz butter into the bowl of an electric mixer fitted with a paddle. Beat on a medium speed for 1 minute, then on high for 1 minute. Scrape down the sides of the bowl, then beat for an additional minute. Scrape down the sides of the bowl, then add the egg and beat on high for 30 seconds. Add the vanilla essence and red raspberry vinegar and beat on high for 20 seconds. Add the melted dark chocolate and mix on a low speed for 10 seconds. Scrape down the sides of the bowl. Now add the sifted dry ingredients and mix on low for 10 seconds.

Increase the speed to medium and beat for 10 seconds. Adjust the speed to low, add the boiling water and continue to mix for 10 seconds. Remove the bowl from the mixer. Use a rubber spatula to mix the batter until smooth and thoroughly combined. (If a table-model electric mixer is not available, follow the directions using a hand-held mixer or mixing by hand. The mixing times will increase depending upon which alternative method is used.)

Evenly divide the batter among the 4 prepared ramekins. Bake in the centre of the oven for 22-25 minutes until a toothpick inserted into the centre of a "bun" comes out clean. Remove from the oven and allow to cool in the cups for 10 minutes. Remove the "buns" from the cups, place upright on a plate, and while still warm, wrap tightly with cling film. Allow to stand at room temperature for at least 1 hour.

Use a very sharp serrated knife or slicer to cut the buns in half horizontally.

The buns are at their best when served at room temperature. They may be refrigerated for 2 or 3 days; remove from the refrigerator about 2 hours before using.

Rubblechuck Fries

Serves 4

125 g/4 oz plain flour
40 g/1½ oz unsalted butter
3 tablespoons water
1 egg yolk, size 3
100 g/3½ oz sugar
1½ teaspoons unsweetened cocoa
½ teaspoon cinnamon

Combine the flour and butter in the bowl of an electric mixer fitted with a paddle. Mix on a medium speed for 2 minutes until the butter is "cut into" the flour. Add the water and egg yolk and continue to mix on a medium speed for 30 seconds. Remove the pastry from the mixer and form it into a smooth ball. Wrap tightly with cling film and refrigerate for 1 hour. (If a table-model electric mixer is not available, follow the directions using a hand-held mixer or kneading by hand. The mixing times will increase depending upon which alternative method is used.)

Preheat the oven to 160°C/325°F/Gas 3.

Lightly sprinkle a clean work surface with some of the sugar. Place the pastry on the surface; use a rolling pin to roll the pastry into a circle about 15 cm/6 in diameter and 1 cm/½ in thick. Sprinkle the cocoa and cinnamon evenly over the pastry and roll into a circle 30 cm/12 in diameter and 0.3 cm/⅛ in thick, using more sugar as necessary to prevent the pastry from sticking. Fold the pastry in half and roll, using more sugar as necessary to prevent the pastry from sticking, into a 40 × 25 cm/16 × 10 in rounded shape that is 0.3 cm/⅛ in thick. Fold and roll once again, using more sugar as necessary to prevent the pastry from sticking, into a 40 × 15 cm/16 × 6 in rectangle that is 0.3 cm/⅛ in thick. At this point, all the sugar should have been used.

Use a sharp knife to cut the pastry into 0.5 cm/¼ in wide strips. Line 2 baking trays with baking parchment. Lay the strips of pastry apart on the baking trays. Bake for 10 to 12 minutes. Remove from the oven and cool to room temperature. Store the fries in an air-tight container to retain crispness.

Rubblechuck *is a slang kitchen term for pastry odds and ends that are rolled with sugar and cinnamon and baked as a special treat for youngsters. Whatever your age, John believes you will love his adaptation.*

Raspberry Relish

Serves 4

50 ml/2 fl oz water
50 g/2 oz sugar
¼ teaspoon finely grated orange rind
225 g/8 oz fresh or frozen raspberries
1 teaspoon fresh orange juice

Heat the water, sugar and orange rind in a saucepan over a medium-high heat. Bring to the boil and allow to boil for 3-4 minutes until slightly thickened. Stir in one-third of the raspberries and continue to boil for 2 minutes.

Remove from the heat and sieve into a small stainless steel bowl. Discard the seeds. Immediately add the remaining raspberries and orange juice. Stir to combine. Refrigerate for at least 30 minutes before serving.

The raspberry relish will keep, tightly covered, in a non-corrosive container for 2 or 3 days.

This relish also makes a great topping for ice cream.

Beef Burger
with Piquant Avocado; Onion, Sage and Mustard Relish; and Fresh Sage Tortillas

Makes 4 burgers

Carl E. Walker
Executive Chef
Brennan's
Houston, Texas

BORN IN FAYETTE, MISSOURI, CHEF CARL WALKER DEVELOPED A PASSION FOR FOOD AND COOKING WHILE GROWING UP ON HIS PARENTS' FARM. THE PRESENCE OF FRESH GAME AND PRODUCE, COMBINED WITH HIS MOTHER'S TALENT IN THE KITCHEN, INSPIRED CARL TO BEGIN EXPLORING THE ART OF COOKING. HE BEGAN HIS FORMAL TRAINING IN THE U.S. MARINE CORPS' COOK'S SCHOOL, WHERE HE GRADUATED FIRST IN HIS CLASS. CARL COMPLETED HIS FORMAL EDUCATION AT THE CULINARY INSTITUTE OF AMERICA.

WITH CHEF CARL WALKER BEHIND THE STOVE, BRENNAN'S HAS RECEIVED A NUMBER OF NOTABLE AWARDS, INCLUDING THE HONOUR OF BEING THE FIRST TEXAS RESTAURANT TO RECEIVE *RESTAURANTS AND INSTITUTIONS* MAGAZINE'S PRESTIGIOUS IVY AWARD.

900 g/2 lb minced beef
150 g/5 oz onions, finely chopped
1 small, hot red or green chilli, roasted, skinned, seeded and finely chopped
2 teaspoons salt
1 teaspoon freshly ground black pepper
4 slices smoked Monterey Jack or smoked Cheddar cheese
2 tablespoons vegetable oil
8 slices ripe red tomatoes

In a large stainless steel bowl, gently but thoroughly combine the minced beef, onions, chilli, salt and pepper.

Gently form the seasoned meat into four 240 g/8½ oz burgers, each 3 cm/1¼ in thick. Cover the burgers with cling film and refrigerate until needed.

Grill the burgers over a medium wood or charcoal fire. Cook as desired: 5-6 minutes on each side for rare, 7-8 minutes on each side for medium and 10-12 minutes on each side for well done. Top each burger with a slice of the smoked cheese and allow to melt. If you have a cover for the grill, quickly melt the cheese by placing it over the grill for a few moments. (This burger may also be cooked on a well-seasoned flat griddle or in a large non-stick frying pan over a medium-high heat. Cook for about the same amount of time as listed for grilling.)

Remove the burgers from the grill. Lightly brush 8 Fresh Sage Tortillas on 1 side with the vegetable oil. Toast the tortillas, oiled sides down, on the grill or griddle or in a non-stick frying pan until lightly browned but still soft.

Spread 2 tablespoons Piquant Avocado on to the grilled side of 4 of the tortillas. Then top each with 2 of the tomato slices and a Beef Burger. Garnish the top of each burger with 1 tablespoon Onion, Sage and Mustard Relish. Place another tortilla, grilled side up, on top. Cut each burger into quarters and serve.

Piquant Avocado

Makes about 250 g/9 oz

2 ripe avocados
1 lemon
1 small hot, red or green chili, roasted, skinned, seeded and finely chopped
³/₄ teaspoon finely chopped fresh coriander
2 dashes Tabasco Sauce
Salt and pepper

Cut, stone and peel the avocados. Cut the avocado pulp into large pieces. Place the avocado pieces into a stainless steel bowl and use the back of a fork to mash them to a coarse texture. Squeeze the juice of the lemon over the mashed avocados. Add the chilli, coriander and Tabasco Sauce to the mashed avocados. Season with salt and pepper. Gently stir to combine. Serve immediately. The Piquant Avocado may be kept, covered, in the refrigerator for several hours.

Onion, Sage and Mustard Relish

Makes about 125 g/4 oz

1¹/₂ teaspoons olive oil
1 large onion, thinly sliced
125 ml/4 fl oz cider vinegar
4 tablespoons sugar
1 tablespoon Dijon mustard
2 teaspoons finely chopped fresh sage
Salt and pepper

Heat the olive oil in a medium frying pan over a medium-high heat. When hot, add the onions and cook for 4 minutes until translucent. Add the cider vinegar and sugar and continue cooking, stirring frequently, for 15-20 minutes until the mixture becomes thick and starts to brown lightly. Remove from the heat and stir in the mustard and sage. Season with salt and pepper and serve immediately.

The relish may be kept warm in a double boiler for up to 1 hour before serving.

To keep the relish for several days, first cool in an ice-water bath, then transfer to a non-corrosive storage container, cover and refrigerate. Heat until warm before serving.

Fresh Sage Tortillas

Makes 8 Tortillas

225 g/8 oz plain flour
2 teaspoons baking powder
2 teaspoons salt
1 teaspoon very finely chopped fresh sage
15 g/¹/₂ oz white vegetable fat
125 ml/4 fl oz warm water, plus 6 tablespoons

In a large stainless steel bowl, sift together the flour, baking powder and salt. Stir in the sage. Rub the white fat into the dry ingredients, then work it in with your hands until the mixture is the consistency of coarse crumbs.

Make a well in the centre of the flour mixture and add 125 ml/4 fl oz warm water. Work the flour in from the sides (add an additional 1 to 6 tablespoons water as needed to get the dough to come together). Gently knead the dough with your hands until it forms a smooth ball.

Cover the bowl with cling film and allow the dough to rest at room temperature for 1 hour.

Remove the dough from the bowl and place it on a lightly floured cutting board. Use a sharp knife to cut the dough into eight 50 g/2 oz pieces. Gently form the pieces into balls, cover loosely with cling film and allow to rest for an additional 15 minutes.

Use a wooden rolling pin to roll each ball into a tortilla about 12.5 cm/5 in in diameter. Wrap the tortillas with cling film and refrigerate until ready to cook. The raw tortillas may be kept refrigerated for up to 4 days.

Mediterranean Lamb Burger

with Tomato and Red Pepper Chutney

Makes 6 burgers

Joseph Weissenberg

Senior Chef-Instructor
The Culinary Institute of America
Hyde Park, New York

SINCE GRADUATING FROM THE CULINARY
INSTITUTE OF AMERICA, JOSEPH
WEISSENBERG HAS CRISS-CROSSED
AMERICA WORKING IN CULINARY
LANDMARKS, INCLUDING THE GOLDEN
LAMB HOTEL IN LEBANON, OHIO, WHERE
HE WAS EXECUTIVE CHEF.

HIS PROUDEST MOMENT, HOWEVER,
WAS IN EUROPE IN 1976, WHEN, AS A
MEMBER OF THE INSTITUTE'S ALUMNI
TEAM, HE WON FIVE GOLD MEDALS AT THE
SALON CULINAIRE MONDIAL IN BASEL,
SWITZERLAND.

THE SIMPLICITY OF JOSEPH'S
MEDITERRANEAN LAMB BURGER BELIES
ITS INTENSITY OF FLAVOUR.

---

*Selecting a beverage to measure up
to the hearty flavour of Joseph's lamb
burger may not be as formidable a task
as one might imagine. Reflect on the
Mediterranean geography that
inspired this burger, and you may find
yourself in the Piedmont region of
Italy, sipping a brawny yet satisfying
Barbaresco in between bites of this
delicious burger.*

**900 g/2 lb fresh lamb meat from
shoulder, trimmed and cut
into 2.5 cm/1 in pieces (or
900 g/2 lb minced lamb
meat from shoulder)**
1 teaspoon salt
**1 teaspoon coarsely ground
black pepper**

6 wholemeal pitta breads
**1 teaspoon extra-virgin
olive oil**
**1 small head curly endive, cut
into bite-size pieces,
washed and dried**

If using lamb pieces, mince them through a meat mincer fitted with a coarse
mincing plate into a large stainless steel bowl.

Gently but thoroughly combine the minced lamb with the salt and pepper.

Gently form the seasoned lamb into six 150 g/5 oz burgers, each 2.5 cm/1 in
thick. Cover the burgers with cling film and refrigerate until needed.

Preheat the oven to 140°C/275°F/Gas 1.

Place the pitta breads on a baking tray and heat in the oven. When hot,
lower the oven temperature to its lowest setting and keep the pitta breads
warm while grilling the lamb burgers.

Lightly brush the burgers with the olive oil.

Grill the burgers over a medium wood or charcoal fire. Cook as desired:
3-4 minutes on each side for rare, 5-6 minutes on each side for medium and
8-9 minutes on each side for well done. (This burger may also be cooked on
a well-seasoned flat griddle or in a large non-stick frying pan over a medium-
high heat. Cook for about the same amount of time as listed for grilling.)

Remove the pitta breads from the oven. Cut a piece from the top of each
pitta bread, then gently split open the bread. Stuff each pitta with curly endive
and a lamb burger. Spoon 2 or 3 teaspoons Tomato and Red Pepper Chutney
directly on to the meat. Serve immediately.

Tomato and Red Pepper Chutney

Makes about 350 g/12 oz

2 **tablespoons olive oil**
4 **spring onions, trimmed and thinly sliced**
1 **small red pepper, seeded and cut into 1 cm/**
½ in dice
1 **clove garlic, very finely chopped**
2 **large tomatoes, peeled, seeded and chopped**
⅛ **teaspoon ground coriander**
⅛ **teaspoon ground cumin**
⅛ **teaspoon ground nutmeg**
⅛ **teaspoon ground turmeric**
Pinch cayenne pepper
1 **tablespoon cider vinegar**
1 **tablespoon sugar**
1 **tablespoon tomato purée**
Salt and cayenne pepper

This condiment is as versatile as your culinary imagination. It works delightfully well with other meats, poultry, and even creatures of the deep—it is terrific served chilled with steamed prawns. Experiment with its serving temperature; it is delicious yet subtly different when served chilled, warm or at room temperature.

Heat the olive oil in a stainless steel saucepan over a medium heat. When hot, add the spring onions, red pepper and garlic. Cook for 2 minutes.

Add the tomatoes and cook for an additional 2 minutes.

Add the ground spices and pinch cayenne pepper and combine thoroughly. Add the cider vinegar and sugar and cook for an additional 2 minutes, occasionally stirring to prevent the mixture scorching.

Add the tomato purée and combine thoroughly. Allow the mixture to simmer for 15 minutes. Remove the chutney from the heat. Adjust the seasoning with salt and additional cayenne pepper, depending on the intensity of heat you prefer.

Cool the chutney in an ice-water bath until cold. Refrigerate the chutney in a stainless steel or other non-corrosive container. Keep refrigerated for 12 hours before serving (this allows the flavours to mingle).

The chutney will keep, tightly covered, in the refrigerator for up to 2 weeks.

Venison Burger

Makes 4 burgers

Jasper White
Chef/Owner
Restaurant Jasper
Boston, Massachusetts

JASPER WHITE HAS ALWAYS BEEN A SUPPORTER OF "THE BASICS OF COOKING" FOR EXAMPLE, HE CONSIDERS A SIMPLE ROASTED CHICKEN AS THE BENCHMARK FOR UNDERSTANDING THE PREPARATION OF GOOD FOOD. AT HIS CELEBRATED RESTAURANT IN BOSTON, JASPER HAS CRAFTED A STYLE OF COOKING THAT HONOURS THE BASICS, YET FAR TRANSCENDS THE ORDINARY.

JASPER, THE AUTHOR OF *JASPER WHITE'S COOKING FROM NEW ENGLAND*, HAS BECOME A SELF-APPOINTED SPOKESMAN FOR THE OFTEN MISUNDERSTOOD AND MISINTERPRETED COOKING OF NEW ENGLAND. HIS VENISON BURGER REFLECTS HIS LONG INTEREST IN HUNTING AND HIS RESPECT FOR NEW ENGLAND'S CUISINE.

> *Although the Venison Burgers are delicious with the condiments recommended above, Jasper suggests that diners "fix up their own burgers" in their own individual ways. Another suggestion from Jasper is to have plenty of dark beer on hand.*

625 g/1¼ lb trimmed venison from shoulder or leg, cut into 2.5 cm/1 in cubes (or 625 g/1¼ lb minced trimmed venison from shoulder or leg)
15 g/½ oz unsalted butter
65 g/2½ oz onion, diced
125 g/ 4 oz pork fat, diced
1 tablespoon olive oil

Salt and coarsely ground black pepper
4 Onion Rolls (see page 89), cut in half
Thinly sliced red onions
Sliced sour pickles
Spicy Dijon mustard
Pepper relish
Tomato and Red Pepper Chutney (see page 133)

If using venison pieces, mince them through a meat mincer fitted with a coarse mincing plate into a large stainless steel bowl. Cover the bowl with cling film and refrigerate until needed.

Heat the butter in a small non-stick frying pan over a medium-high heat. When hot, add the onions and cook for 3-4 minutes until translucent. Transfer onions to a plate and place, uncovered, in the refrigerator.

Combine the minced venison with the pork fat and cooled onions.

Gently form the meat-onion mixture into four 175 g/6 oz burgers, each 2.5 cm/1 in thick. Cover the burgers with cling film and refrigerate until needed.

Prior to grilling, brush the Venison Burgers with the olive oil and generously season with salt and pepper.

Grill the burgers over a medium wood or charcoal fire. Cook as desired: 3-4 minutes on each side for medium rare, 5-6 minutes on each side for medium and 8-9 minutes on each side for well done. (This burger may also be cooked on a well-seasoned flat griddle or in a large non-stick frying pan over a medium-high heat. Cook for about the same amount of time as listed for grilling.)

Remove the burgers from the grill. Toast the rolls, cut sides down, on the grill or griddle or in a non-stick frying pan until golden brown. Place each burger on the bottom half of a roll.

Top the burgers with the red onion slices, sour pickle slices, mustard, pepper relish, Tomato and Red Pepper Chutney and top bun halves.

Chilli Grill Burger

with Chilli Cheddar Buns, Chilli Mayonnaise and Grilled Vegetables Prickly Pear

Makes 4 burgers

Alan Zeman
Executive Chef
Sheraton El Conquistador Resort
Tucson, Arizona

CONSIDERED BY MANY TO BE TUCSON'S AMBASSADOR OF SOUTH-WEST CUISINE, ALAN ZEMAN HAS BEEN HOOKED ON THE CITY'S SUNSHINE AND MOUNTAINS SINCE HE MOVED THERE TO ATTEND THE UNIVERSITY OF ARIZONA IN 1975. WHILE STUDYING, HE WORKED HIS WAY THROUGH THE FINER HOTELS AND RESTAURANTS OF THE TUCSON AREA. FINDING THAT HE HAD A GREATER AFFINITY FOR THE KITCHEN THAN FOR POLITICAL SCIENCE, ALAN DECIDED TO ATTEND THE CULINARY INSTITUTE OF AMERICA.

AS ONE OF THE ARCHITECTS OF THE NEW SOUTH-WEST CUISINE, ALAN DEVELOPED THE ORIGINAL PRICKLY PEAR BARBECUE GLAZE, MARKETED HIS OWN SONORAN SEASONING AND IS WIDELY REGARDED AS THE INVENTOR OF THE DESSERT TACO.

ALAN'S INNOVATIVE SKILLS BRING THE SOUTH-WEST RIGHT TO THE PALATE WITH HIS CHILLI GRILL BURGER.

---

900 g/2 lb minced beef
1 tablespoon seasoned salt
4 large, mild green chillies, roasted, skinned and seeded

4 slices Monterey Jack cheese or Cheddar cheese
4 Iceberg lettuce leaves, washed and dried
4 slices ripe large tomatoes

Gently form the minced beef into four 225 g/8 oz burgers, each 3 cm/1¼ in thick. Cover the burgers with cling film and refrigerate until needed.

Generously season the burgers with the seasoned salt. Grill the burgers over a medium wood or charcoal fire. Cook as desired: 3-4 minutes on each side for rare, 6-7 minutes on each side for medium and 8-9 minutes on each side for well done. (This burger may also be cooked on a well-seasoned flat griddle or in a large non-stick frying pan. Cook for about the same amount of time as listed for grilling.) As soon as the burgers have been cooked on one side and are turned, place 2 of the large mild green chilli halves on the grilled side of each burger and then place a slice of the cheese on the chillies. Finish cooking as desired.

Remove the burgers from the grill. Cut 4 Chilli Cheddar Buns in half. Toast the buns on the grill or griddle or in a non-stick frying pan, cut sides down, until golden brown. Place the burgers on the bottom bun halves and top with the lettuce and tomatoes. Spread the top bun halves with 1 tablespoon Chilli Mayonnaise and place on top of the burgers. Serve immediately with Grilled Vegetables Prickly Pear.

Alan has been known to wash a burger down with an ice-cold beer that has the body to stand up to the bold flavours of the Chilli Grill Burger.

Chilli Cheddar Buns

Makes 12 buns

450 ml/³/₄ pint milk
2 tablespoons sugar
2 teaspoons salt
2 tablespoons dried yeast
800 g/26 oz plain flour
250 g/9 oz Cheddar cheese, grated
2 eggs, size 3
50 ml/2 fl oz vegetable oil, plus 1 teaspoon
3 medium, hot green or red chillies, stalks removed, seeded and finely chopped

Heat the milk, sugar and salt in a saucepan over a medium heat to a temperature of 50°C/120°F. Remove from the heat and pour into the bowl of an electric mixer. Add the yeast and stir gently to dissolve. Allow the mixture to stand and foam for 4–5 minutes.

Add 750 g/1¹/₂ lb of the flour, 225 g/8 oz of the cheese, the eggs, 50 ml/2 fl oz vegetable oil and the chillies. Place the mixing bowl on an electric mixer fitted with a dough hook. Mix on a low speed for 1 minute. Stop the mixer, scrape down the sides of the bowl and continue mixing on a medium-low speed for 4–5 minutes until the dough forms a smooth ball that pulls away from the sides of the bowl. (If a table-model electric mixer is not available, follow the directions using a hand-held mixer or kneading by hand. The mixing times will increase depending upon which alternative method is used.)

Coat the inside of a large stainless steel bowl with the remaining teaspoon vegetable oil. Place the dough in the bowl and wipe the bowl with the dough. Cover with cling film. Allow the dough to rise in a warm location for 1 hour until it has doubled in volume.

Preheat the oven to 160°C/325°F/Gas 3.

Place the dough on a clean, lightly floured work surface, using the remaining flour as necessary. Use a sharp knife to cut the dough into 12 equal portions. Shape each portion into a ball. Divide the balls on to 2 baking trays lined with baking parchment. Slightly flatten the top of each ball. Loosely cover the dough with cling film and allow to rise in a warm location for 20 minutes, or until doubled in size.

When the buns have doubled in size, use a razor blade or a very sharp paring knife to cut a 1 cm/¹/₂ in deep slit in the top of each bun. Sprinkle the remaining Cheddar over the top of the buns. Bake the buns in the centre of the oven for 23–25 minutes until golden brown.

Allow the buns to cool thoroughly before cutting in half.

The rolls will keep fresh for 2 or 3 days at room temperature stored in a sealed polythene bag.

Chilli Mayonnaise

Makes about 250 g/9 oz

**2 small, dried, hot red or green chillies, stalks
  removed and seeded (see Note)**
225 g/8 oz mayonnaise
2 teaspoons white wine
1 teaspoon Worcestershire sauce
1 teaspoon seasoned salt
1 teaspoon finely chopped garlic

Use the edge of a cook's knife to press the chillies into a
paste to make about 1 teaspoon paste.

In a stainless steel bowl, whisk together the mayonnaise, chilli paste, white wine, Worcestershire sauce, seasoned salt and garlic. Use immediately or cover with
cling film and refrigerate for up to 2 days.

Note: Make sure you use dried chillies in this recipe.

Grilled Vegetables Prickly Pear

Serves 4

**1 courgette, washed and cut into 0.5 cm/¹/₄ in
  slices**
**1 yellow squash, washed and cut into 0.5 cm/
  ¹/₄ in slices**
**1 aubergine, washed and cut into 0.5 cm/¹/₄ in
  slices**
8 spring onions, trimmed
125 ml/4 fl oz extra-virgin olive oil
2 tablespoons seasoned salt
**175 ml/6 fl oz Quick Barbecue Sauce (see page
  46), or a favourite barbecue sauce**

Prior to grilling, brush the vegetables with the olive oil
and season generously with the seasoned salt. Grill the
courgette and yellow squash over a medium wood or
charcoal fire for about 1¹/₂ minutes on each side. Grill the
aubergine for 45–60 seconds on each side. Grill the whole
spring onions for about 30 seconds.

Transfer the grilled vegetables to a serving platter; brush
liberally with barbecue sauce. Serve immediately.

The grilled vegetables may be kept warm in a 100°C/
200°F/Gas Low oven for up to 30 minutes before serving.
The vegetables are also good at room temperature; cover
with cling film and keep for up to 1 hour at room temperature before serving.

Note: If you cannot find a barbecue glaze with a
prickly pear fruit base, use your favourite barbecue sauce.

 # Index

More Good Food and Words from the American Burger Masters

Desaulniers, Marcel. *The Trellis Cookbook.* New York: Weidenfeld & Nicolson, 1988.

———. *Death by Chocolate: The Last Word on a Consuming Passion.* New York: Rizzoli, International Publications, 1992.

———. *The Trellis Cookbook.* Expanded edition. New York: Simon and Schuster, Fireside Paperbacks, 1992.

Fearing, Dean. *The Mansion on Turtle Creek Cookbook.* New York: Weidenfeld and Nicolson, 1987.

———. *Dean Fearing's Southwest Cuisine: Blending Asia and the Americas.* New York: Grove Weidenfeld, 1990.

Garvin, Kevin. *Seasoned in Texas.* Dallas: Taylor Publishing Company, 1992.

Lang, Jenifer. *Tastings: The Best from Ketchup to Caviar.* New York: Crown Publishers, 1986.

———. *Jenifer Lang Cooks for Kids.* New York: Crown Publishers, Harmony Books, 1991.

Leader, Daniel. *Bread Alone.* New York: William Morrow and Company, 1993.

Routhier, Nicole. *Foods of Vietnam.* New York: Stewart, Tabori & Chang, 1989.

———. *Cooking Under Wraps.* New York: William Morrow and Company, 1993.

Schlesinger, Chris. *The Thrill of the Grill.* New York: William Morrow and Company, 1990.

White, Jasper. *Jasper White's Cooking from New England.* New York: Harper and Row Publishers, 1989.